THE POWER OF INTERCESSION

The Power of Intercession

Effective Prayer for the Needs of Others

Peter Grant

SERVANT BOOKS
Ann Arbor, Michigan

Cover photo by John B. Leidy copyright © 1984 by
Servant Publications.
Book design by John B. Leidy

Available from Servant Publications, Box 8617,
Ann Arbor, Michigan 48107

ISBN 0-89283-132-4
Printed in the United States of America

Most scripture quotations in this book are from the Revised
Standard Version, copyright 1946, 1952 © 1971, 1973 by the
Division of Christian Education of the National Council of the
Churches of Christ in the U.S.A.

84 85 86 87 88 89 10 9 8 7 6 5 4 3

Contents

Introduction

THE HOLY SPIRIT IS BRINGING various ministries into prominence in the church today. Gifts such as tongues, prophecy, and healing, which seemed to be dormant for centuries, are once again being accorded their rightful place within the overall ministry of the Body of Christ. However, less dramatic ministries which are indispensable to the work of the church which have been present in the Church since its earliest days. One such ministry is intercession.

Most of us have practiced intercessory prayer for those close to us and for situations we are involved in. However, there is another dimension to intercession, which has in the past been chiefly recognized and practiced by the contemplative religious orders. This is committed intercession as a vocation and a ministry in itself. Today, Christians in every walk of life are becoming aware of the need for dedicated intercessors to provide spiritual support and enrichment for the church's life.

This book is aimed primarily at those involved in, or interested in, the ministry of intercession. It can be of use to anyone wishing to know more about intercession in general terms as well. Each chapter is designed as a separate "study unit," which can be used on its own, for use in individual or group study.

I am deeply grateful for the support and encouragement I have received from my brothers and sisters in Christ during the writing of this book. Among those who gave generously of their time and talents were the Noffke family, Fr. Gregory Brooke, O.P., Peter Norval, and Hugo Potgieter. My parents were always a tower of strength, and made several valuable suggestions. I'd also like to thank Jim Manney of Servant

Books for his advice and patience. Finally, my thanks go especially to a woman who was, in a very real way, responsible for the beginnings of my own commitment to the ministry of intercession. She has become widely known and loved throughout the Body of Christ in South Africa, and her ministry of writing and teaching has been well received. This book is therefore dedicated, with warm Christian love, to Dot Mitchell.

PETER GRANT
CAPE TOWN, SOUTH AFRICA

APRIL 1983

ONE

Petition, Mediation, and Intercession

I WOULD DISTINGUISH between three kinds of what we might term "asking" prayer. These are *petitionary* prayer, prayer of *mediation,* and *intercessory* prayer. Intercession can be further divided into two categories: the general intercessory prayer to which all Christians are called, and the more committed ministry of intercession. Let's examine each of these types of prayer in turn.

We are familiar with petitionary prayer. This is prayer for our own needs, and for the needs of groups with which we are directly connected. It includes prayer for solutions to problems, for help in difficult situations, for material needs, and so on. All Christians are enabled to exercise this form of prayer, and are called upon to "have no anxiety about anything, but in everything by prayer and supplication with thanksgiving let your requests be made known to God" (Phil 4:6).

Prayer of mediation is more difficult to define. The boundary between this form of prayer and intercession is often blurred to the point of being almost nonexistent. I see prayer of mediation as being that prayer which is offered *with,* or *in the presence of,* the person or persons for whom we pray, at times when we seek to act as direct, physically present channels of God's grace to them. Within this category I would include prayer for physical and inner healing, the ministry of deliverance, and — to a limited extent — so-called "word gifts" like prophecy. We might well ask why it is necessary to differentiate between mediation and intercession in view of their similarity. The reason that I prefer to do so is that intercession is, in most cases, offered in the absence of the person or group for whom we are praying, and has a much wider scope.

As well as being offered for individuals and groups of people, intercession deals with every situation in the world that needs the support of prayer. We intercede *for* nations, ministries, church groups, victims of natural and man-made disasters, for peace and stability; we pray *against* the disruptive influence of the devil and his servants, the greed and rapacity of mankind, and similar evils. Of the three forms of prayer, it can be seen that intercession embraces far more numerous and diverse areas than do mediation or petition.

As mentioned earlier, intercession can be divided into two areas. The first of these is the ordinary, everyday intercession that all Christians are called upon to offer. This category includes prayer for one's family, work, home, and church, and for temporal and spiritual leaders. It is unfortunate, indeed tragic, that many of us neglect these basic intercessory responsibilties. Imagine the power of prayer that would be unleashed if, for example, every Christian in a city were to pray for the mayor and city council on a regular, committed basis: even the most pagan of administrations might be transformed in a short time. We all need to take careful stock of how we are meeting these everyday calls to intercession, and to mend our ways where this proves necessary.

The second form of intercession is what we will be primarily concerned with in this book—although, of course, one can apply most of what is said here to "general" intercession as well. This second form is what I would call "ministry" intercession. This is the intercession offered by an individual or group who have been called by God to commit themselves to regular, in-depth intercession as an expression of their

Christian lives and ministry. Such a commitment to intercession is a ministry in itself, along with such better-known areas
as healing, prophecy, and discernment. In fact, one who is
committed to the ministry of intercession will often find is
elements of these other ministries become manifest in his or
her own life. Because of the need of the intercessor to remain
closely attuned to God's will in directing his or her prayers, a
greater awareness of the movements of the Holy Spirit is
generated. This greater openness naturally enables one to be
used by God for many other gifts, as well as for effective and
powerful intercession.

Who is called to this ministry? In my own case, I did not
realize that I had been called to committed intercession until I
had already been engaged in it for a few years. One is drawn
into it gradually, as with most other ministries in the Body of
Christ. Some intercessors have, indeed, received explicit and
direct calls from God to enter this ministry, but in general,
confirmation comes as the passage of time demonstrates the
effectiveness of one's prayers, and as the Christian community
is able to observe one's intercessory activity.

Many people today have not found any particular spiritual
or pastoral activity through which to express their Christian
commitment more fully. I should like to suggest to such
people that they examine the ministry of intercession more
closely.This ministry is among the most important services
that any Christian can offer, both to God and to fellow
believers—not to mention the world around us. Intercessory
prayer is like the fuel pump of a car. A car can have a tank full of
gasoline, but unless there is a pump to draw the petrol from
the tank to the motor, it won't get very far. In the same way, the
church of God has the power of the Holy Spirit available to it.
To enable this power to touch and revitalize those areas where
it is needed, God has given us the gift of intercessory prayer.
This is not to suggest that the Lord cannot or will not move in
power if we do not pray. However, he has commissioned us to

be the instruments of his love on this earth. Weak and frail though we are, he has given us the gift of his Spirit, and has sent us out as "a chosen race, a royal priesthood, a holy nation, God's own people, that you may declare the wonderful deeds of him who called you out of darkness into his marvelous light" (1 Pt 2:9). This proclamation of God's love cannot be based on words alone. Jesus preached his Good News by deeds as well as words, and we are called upon to do the same. While some people are placed in situations where they are able to demonstrate the grace of God in direct action, others of us do not have this opportunity. No matter what our situation in life, however, we are still able to assist God's work through our intercession for people and situations that are in need of divine help. Our task is no less important than that of the most active and inspired preachers and teachers of the church.

Many of the most effective intercessors I have met have been housewives and others who do not work set hours in an office or factory. They are better able to set time aside in their daily schedules for regular, committed intercession, as individuals or in groups. Others, like myself, have to exercise this ministry in different ways, and must make time for prayer whenever opportunity offers. I believe that no one can honestly say that he or she is too busy to find time for intercessory prayer (in addition, of course, to their normal personal prayer). It's a well-known saying that "if you're too busy to pray, then you're too busy!" Whatever our method of prayer, and whatever the time we devote to our intercession, we can be certain that our ministry is a vital lifeline of spiritual support to every area of the church's work. In fact, I seriously doubt whether any of the activities of the body of Christ could bear much fruit without regular, committed prayer support.

We should remember, at this point, those men and women who have chosen to devote their entire lives to prayer and intercession. These monks, nuns, priests, and brothers of the so-called "contemplative" religious orders are often maligned. Many would rather see them engaged in what they call "truly **active** ministry to and in the Body of Christ." How wrong such people are! These contemplatives form a powerhouse of prayer, generating spiritual support and blessing for the more physically active areas of the church's ministry. Without them, we would be in dire straits. I believe that their task is perhaps the most demanding and the most important in the church today. Let us give them all respect and honor for their faithfulness and devotion, and praise and thank God for their response to his call. Such a vocation demands incredible self-sacrifice and humility, and few of us would have the courage to accept such a lifestyle if we were called upon to do so.

There are also various groups of lay people, particularly within the Catholic Church, who have vowed themselves to a life of prayer, intercession, and Christian witness while living in the midst of normal society. Some take vows of celibacy as well, so as to free themselves for greater involvement in their apostolate. The men and women of these so-called "secular institutes" also deserve far greater recognition than is generally given to them. One is often unaware of their presence in society, or in one's local church; yet their quiet, unassuming service of intercession and pastoral labor is a vital ingredient of the church's everyday life.

We have looked briefly at the role of intercessory prayer in the wider ministry of the Body of Christ. Now let's look at the way in which the concept of intercession developed in scripture, and then go on to consider each aspect of intercessory prayer in more detail.

TWO

Prayer and Intercession in the Old Testament

IN ORDER TO CORRECTLY ASSESS the development of intercession in the Old Testament, we should first examine the
overall scope of the prayer of Israel, and the way in which it
developed. One can immediately see that the concepts of
prayer and sacrifice were very closely linked. If an individual
(or, indeed, the whole nation) wished to "seek Yahweh," he (or
they) did so through sacrifice, in prayer. Hosea, for example,
speaks of Israel going "with their flocks and herds . . . to seek
the Lord" (Hos 5:6), although on this occasion, he tells them,
it will be wasted effort. The Old Testament mentions many
elements in the overall concept of prayer—to glorify and
praise God, to petition him for one's needs, to intercede on
behalf of others, to entreat, to propitiate—as well as various
bodily postures used in prayer—standing, kneeling, lying
prostrate, bowing the head upon the knees, lifting or stretch-
ing out the hands, and so on.

A noteworthy characteristic of Old Testament prayer is that
it is exclusively directed to Yahweh, the one God of Israel. This
separates it from the prayers of contemporary pagan religions,
which were directed to many gods. Yahweh is the God of the
Covenant, and Israel is his chosen people; any Israelite can
approach God directly because of the covenant relationship

7

between them. Only after the Exile do we find mention in the Old Testament of angels acting as mediators for prayer between God and man (Zec 1:12; Jb 5:1; Dn 12:1; Tb 12:15). The petitioner's complete confidence in God, based upon Yahweh's unwavering faithfulness to the covenant he has initiated, is expressed in various ways in the Old Testament. God is his "rock," his "refuge," his "stronghold," his "shield"; examples of these expressions abound, especially in the Psalms. God's omnipotence is one of the major reasons for placing total trust in him; "our help is in the name of the Lord, who made heaven and earth" (Ps 124:8; cf. Pss 8, 19, 29, 104, 147, etc.).

The Israelite was discouraged from using many words, or repeating formulas, when he addressed Yahweh (Eccl 5:1-2; Sir 7:14; cf. Mt 6:7). The use by pagans of incantations and long-winded prayers is seen as a clear indication of their lack of trust in, and respect for, their deities. Hebrew prayer does not directly apply pressure on God to alter his will, although at times it becomes quite importunate, as if seeking an answer to the dilemma in which the petitioner finds himself. It seeks, and at times comes close to demanding, enlightenment from God as to why he is taking a particular course of action or withholding his support. (Again, there are good examples of this in the Psalter.) Often the prayer is humble, seeking forgiveness as well as help. The lack of pomposity in Israelite prayer is very noticeable.

The Old Testament stresses liturgical or public prayer, which involves the entire community of Israel, and places little emphasis on private prayer. Prayer could, however, be offered anywhere, and was not limited to the Temple (although in later years, especially after the Exile, sacrifice was restricted to the Temple in Jerusalem). According to some writers, the whole of Israel was regarded as the sanctuary of Yahweh in the midst of a heathen world. There is an element of mysticism in the visions of the prophets and in some other passages recorded in the scriptures, and this element was probably carried over into the prayers of some individuals. The will of Yahweh was seen as being the salvation of Israel, and was not static, but dynamic. When the Israelite prayed, he struggled in prayer as if involved in a flesh-and-blood battle, striving to attain to a life filled with the active power of God.

We can now look more closely at the petitionary prayer of Israel, which will, in turn, lead us to consider the more specifically intercessory prayers found in the Old Testament. The Hebrew mentality did not consider abstract thought or concepts such as the possibility of life after death. The Jews had not separated material and spiritual values, as we have today, nor had they removed these values from their everyday environment. "Peace," for example, which we would generally regard as a "spiritual" good in our own lives, was an eminently practical and material good to them. (This is not, of course, to suggest that it cannot be equally practical and material to us; but today we can distinguish between inner peace of mind, and peace between, for example, warring nations. (The Old Testament does not make such a distinction.)Israelite supplication was concerned with benefits such as prosperity, riches, and long life. Prayers are also recorded requesting benefits such as wisdom, forgiveness of sins, preservation from error. Often the Israelites prayed blessings—and, indeed, curses—on others. At times, all of Israel sought Yahweh collectively in order to draw his attention to the needs of his people, and to implore his aid. There are many examples of these forms of petition to be found in the Old Testament. Especially in the Psalms, I have found tremendous depths of prayer, and I recommend that anyone serious about prayer should begin by studying them.

Now let us turn to a more specific examination of intercessory prayer in the Old Testament. There are many Hebrew words and phrases used to explain the part played by the intercessor. His role is to "step into the gap on behalf of Israel" (Ez 13:5, 22:30; Ps 106:23), and to "build a wall around the people" (Ez 13:5, 22:30). These and similar phrases indicate the duty of the intercessor to "stand between" Yahweh and Israel, and to plead Israel's cause with him. The intercessor is one who prays to God for someone else, acting as an intermediary or mediator (Ex 8:8, 9:8; Nm 12:13) in order to cause God to show mercy or favor towards those for whom he is praying (Ex 32:11-14; Jer 26:19).

In the Psalms, we see many examples of intercessory prayer, especially for Jerusalem (Ps 122, among others), and for the king (there are many examples of this, including such well-known references as Ps 20 and Ps 61:6-7). In the Lamentations of Jeremiah, we find intercession for the restoration of Israel and the averting of calamity (Lam 5), and there are similar prayers in the Psalter. These are all essentially the prayers of the community of Israel, pleading its cause before God; but they could also be used as prayers of intercession prayed on behalf of the people by an individual.

In the Wisdom literature, very little is said specifically about intercessory prayer, but there are scattered references (Jb 42:8; Sir 45:23-24). For the first time, mention is made of intercession by heavenly beings, angels praying on behalf of man (Jb 5:1, 33:23-26). The book of Daniel also mentions angels as God's messengers, bringing answers to prayer (Dn 9:22-23, 10:12) or interpreting prophetic visions (Dn 8:15-16). At the end of the Old Testament, we find intercession for the dead (2 Mc 12:40-45) and for pagans (2 Mc 3:31-33). There is a clear development in the understanding of the role of the intercessor; the early view saw him as praying alone to God on behalf of others, but this developed until he was seen as praying to God for himself also, as one of the group for whom he was making intercession—in other words, he was now identified completely with the cause for which he was interceding. (For an illustration of this, see Daniel 9:4-19). However, one unchanging requirement was that the person or group for whom intercession was being made should have the correct attitude of openness to God, and a willingness to accept his lordship. Indeed, Yahweh specifically forbade

Jeremiah to intercede before him on behalf of Israel, because of their wrong attitudes (Jer 14:11-12).

There are many individuals who acted as intercessors in the Old Testament, and we shall now examine several of them in detail. In this limited space we cannot examine them all; we shall select certain individuals and look at their intercessory role more closely. We shall begin with Abraham, "the father of all who believe" (Rom 4:11; cf. Gal 3:6-7).

Abraham is the first major biblical figure who intercedes with God on behalf of others. He asks God to spare the city of Sodom and its inhabitants, in a famous dialogue during which God promises to spare the city if only a certain number of just men (which is eventually reduced to ten) are found there (Gn 18:22-33). He also intercedes with God on behalf of Abimelech, after Abimelech had taken away Abraham's wife Sarah, believing her to be Abraham's sister (Gn 20:1-17). Here God is shown to be open to Abraham's plea, because of the love he bears for his servant and the covenant that exists between them (cf. Sir 44:19-21).

In Moses, we have the supreme example of the intercessor in the Old Testament. Indeed, Moses is portrayed as the prophet, intercessor, mediator, military and political leader, and priest par excellence. As the closing words of the book of Deuteronomy eulogize him:

> "And there has not arisen a prophet since in Israel like Moses, whom the Lord knew face to face, none like him for all the signs and wonders which the Lord sent him to do in the land of Egypt, to Pharaoh and to all his servants and to all his land, and for all the mighty power and all the great and terrible deeds which Moses wrought in the sight of all Israel." (Dt 34:10-12)

Moses intercedes both for individuals and for the people of Israel as a whole (Dt 9:18-20, 25-29). During the plagues in Egypt, he intercedes with God on behalf of Pharaoh to end the plagues (Ex 8:8-13, for example). In the desert, when a fire threatens the Israelites, he again intercedes with the Lord for protection and relief from danger (Nm 11:1-2), and when Yahweh is angry with his rebellious people, Moses pleads with him for forbearance, reminding the Lord of his love and mercy (cf. Nm 14:10b-20; Ex 32:7-14). As one innocent of Israel's sin of idolatry, he pleads with Yahweh for forgiveness of their sin (Ex 32:30-34). During the events surrounding the making of the Covenant at Sinai, the people are so afraid at the awesome sight that they plead with Moses to stand between them and the cloud (Ex 20:18-21). In Moses, therefore, the Old Testament authors portray a man who is at home with God to such an extent that he can sway God's wrath and produce mercy instead: a man with great powers of intercession.

Many of the prophets acted as intercessors also; indeed, one of the signs of a genuine prophet was his intercession. In the earliest of the prophetic books, the prophet Amos interceded for his people in the face of God's wrath (Am 7:1-6). Indeed, one of Ezekiel's chief criticisms of the false prophets of his time is that they failed to intercede for Israel in prayer (Ez 13:3-5, 22:28-31). There are several recorded incidents of people turning to a "man of God" and seeking his intercession (for example, 2 Kgs 19:2-4; Jer 21:1-2). The prophets needed to be purified from the sinfulness of the people, as Isaiah was (Is 6:1-13). Micah also bemoaned the sinfulness of his people, with whom he identified himself when reminding his listeners of God's mercy (Mi 7:19).

Jeremiah is one of the most powerful intercessors in the whole of the Old Testament. He is the representative of the people and their rulers before God (Jer 21:1-2, 37:3, 42:1-4), and he identifies himself with the sin of Israel in his prayer of intercession (Jer 14:7-9, 19-22). However, God refuses to listen to his prayer on behalf of the people, because they do not follow his ways and do not have the right attitudes towards him. After Jeremiah's death and the return of the Jews from exile, he was remembered as an unceasing intercessor for Israel (2 Mc 15:12-16).

Ezekiel, on the other hand, does not identify himself with the wrongdoing of Israel, but acts and speaks as one outside their sin. He amplifies and extends a very important concept mentioned in Jeremiah 31:29-30, namely, that of individual, not collective, responsibility for sin. He rejects the old doctrine that "the sins of the fathers shall be visited upon their sons," and instead stresses the fact that each individual is answerable to God for his own sins (Ez 14:12-23, 18:1-32, 33:10-20). These attitudes influenced his prayer for Israel and affected those who followed him. As previously mentioned, he castigates the false prophets for their failure to intercede for Israel.

The four Songs of the Servant of Yahweh, in the second part of the book of Isaiah, present very interesting concepts of the "servant of Yahweh" (Is 42:1-4, 49:1-6, 50:4-9, and 52:13-53:12). The Servant of God (who is a foreshadowing of the Son of God, Jesus the Christ) is portrayed as a powerful intercessor and mediator of God's will. He embodies, in himself, the covenant that God has made with man, and is a savior and king in his own right. As Isaiah 53:12 puts it, "he bore the sin of many, and made intercession for the transgressors." We shall see in the next chapter how Jesus fulfills these types.

The Old Testament depicts the early development and practice of intercessory prayer, and gives many examples of intercession and intercessors. We can learn much from them, and, in our study of the development of intercessory prayer in the New Testament, we shall discover that all of the new and amplified ideas expressed in the gospels and epistles rely on the foundations laid in the Old Testament. The teachings of the New Testament on intercessory prayer reinforce and expand the lessons of the Old, and the two should be studied together, so that this mutual support and development can be fully appreciated.

THREE

The Intercession of Christ in the Gospels

I N THIS CHAPTER, we shall examine the way in which Christ interceded for his followers with his Father in prayer, and also examine his words concerning the Holy Spirit as intercessor. To grasp fully the place of Christ's intercession within the scope of his total prayer life, one should really have a fairly detailed knowledge of the prayers he made, the times and places of his prayer, and so on. Anyone seriously interested in the ministry of intercession should devote much time, prayer, and study to becoming far better acquainted with Jesus' prayer life. I should like to recommend a short book on this subject, *To Pray as Jesus,* by George Martin (Servant Books, 1978).

Let us, then, briefly examine the prayer life of Jesus. There is a very important dual element in his prayer; he prays both as a devout Jew, and as the divine Son of God. Jesus used all the prayers, psalms, and songs of praise common to Judaism. At the Last Supper, he and the Twelve probably sang or recited the great "Hallel" psalmody of thanksgiving (Ps 113-118), as was traditional before the Passover. He was a regular attender at the services in the synagogues (Mt 9:35, 13:54; Mk 1:21; Lk 4:16; etc.). As a pious Jew, he would have known, and daily prayed, the Shema (Dt 6:4-7), as all Jews were obliged to do. The influence of his divine Sonship is also evident in his prayer.

He prayed before every major event, crisis, or occurrence in his earthly ministry: during his miracles (for example, Mk 6:41 or Jn 6:11), at his baptism (Lk 3:21), or before choosing the Twelve (Lk 6:12). In the Garden of Gethsemane, he struggled in prayer, seeking release from the burden of fear and weakness which he felt (Mt 26:36-46). He remained in prayer for whole nights, at times; indeed, we may say that Jesus' entire life was lived in intimate union with God, and it was from this union, visibly expressed in his prayers, that his life and ministry drew their vitality and power. This may sound like an obvious thing to say, but how often do we think of it?

There are few occasions in the gospels where Christ prays in a specifically intercessory manner; we shall consider these shortly. Let us, before coming to these, examine the statement by Jesus to the effect that he who openly proclaims Jesus to the world will be accepted by him and proclaimed as his in heaven (see Mt 10:32-33; Mk 8:38; Lk 9:26; and Lk 12:8-9). From the passage given in Matthew 10:32-33, which appears to me to be the clearest, we can see that at the last judgment, Jesus will speak up, or intercede, before the Father on behalf of those who have followed him faithfully on earth. On the other hand, all those who have denied or rejected Christ during their earthly lives will find him standing as a prosecutor or accuser before God. There are two important conclusions which may be drawn from these passages. One, more immediately evident, is that eternal salvation is dependent on man's response to God in the "here and now"; but more important from the point of view of the intercessor is that the presentation of a cause by Jesus before his Father, either as accuser or defender, seems final and irrevocable. He is the final, ultimate intercessor, and it would seem that once he has taken a stand on behalf of, or against, a person before his Father, nothing changes the effect of his decision.

In the Gospel of Luke, we see Jesus interceding for Peter before the ordeal of the Garden of Gethsemane (Lk 22:31-32). Here we see a parallel in the actions of the Enemy, Satan; as he had asked God to be allowed to test the faith of Job (Jb 1:6-12, 2:1-6), so now he asks to be allowed to attack Peter, and to test him. Jesus, however, says here that he has interceded on Peter's behalf, so that he should not be completely overcome—although he realizes that Peter will fall initially, before his recovery. Christ's intercession is not made merely to strengthen Peter, but so that Peter, once he has "turned again," will be in a position to strengthen and lead the other apostles. Here, Jesus intercedes on behalf of his most faithful followers.

Jesus teaches us, both by word and example, to intercede for our enemies and not to bear malice towards them in our hearts. In Matthew 5:44-45, we are told to "love your enemies and pray for those who persecute you, so that you may be sons of your Father who is in heaven." Christ directly links our relationship as children of the Father with our intercession for our enemies. He himself fulfilled this command on the Cross, when he prayed for his executioners, and for those who had had a hand in bringing about his death: "Father, forgive them, for they know not what they do" (Lk 23:34). In the Acts of the Apostles, Stephen also prayed for his murderers in this fashion (Acts 7:60).

The most prolonged prayer of intercession made by Jesus is found in the seventeenth chapter of the Gospel of John—the so-called "High Priestly Prayer of Jesus." He prays to his Father for the preservation of his apostles, and asks that they be bound together in a unity and love as great as that which unites him with the Father. He asks that they may be "consecrated in truth." Here we should remember that in the Hebrew mentality prayer and sacrifice were intimately linked. Jesus has prayed that his followers should be strengthened and preserved; now he states that "for their sake I consecrate myself, that they also may be consecrated in truth" (cf. Jn 17:19). Just as an animal for sacrificial use was consecrated to God before being sacrificed, so Jesus now consecrates himself as the sacrifice to be offered for his followers. This passage has a great deal to say to us as intercessors. Are we able to pray so deeply and so profoundly for something or someone, and to desire the fulfillment and accomplishment of our prayer so strongly, that we are prepared to offer our very lives to God as a sacrifice for the completion of that work? This should be the essence of true intercession; that we lay down our lives in prayer, so that God's plan and purpose in and for the world, and all who live in it, may be fulfilled. Intercession is no light thing, no laughing matter. It is one of the most serious commitments we can ever make in our Christian lives; and if we sincerely wish our intercession to be completely fruitful, then we should be prepared to enter into this sacrificial, all-consuming commitment to act as instruments of prayer in the hand of God.

In the Letter to the Hebrews, the author shows the theological development of the idea of Jesus as the new and eternal High Priest, and we see a well-developed understanding of the intercessory role of the now glorified Christ. Hebrews 7:25 says of Christ that "he is able for all time to save those who draw near to God through him, since he always lives to make intercession for them." Christ is himself the sacrifice offered for our sins; and, having *been* sacrificed, he becomes also the High Priest, who *offers* sacrifice. It is his chief priestly function to intercede for his followers (cf. Rom 8:34).

Having examined the actual intercession of Christ, let us now see what we, as intercessors, may glean from the host of other things said by him concerning our prayer life in general, and our relationship with God. I have derived much personal benefit from detailed study of the relevant scripture texts, using them as a source of personal meditation and prayer, and I recommend the same to anyone interested in developing their understanding of intercessory prayer. Only by "personalizing" these things, and situating them in the context of one's own life and circumstances, can one derive real benefit from them.

Christ teaches his disciples to pray, and this prayer, which we commonly call the "Our Father," or "The Lord's Prayer" contains many elements that we, as intercessors, should bear in mind. It contains seven petitions in the version presented in the Gospel of Matthew; the first three concern God himself, and the last four deal with the needs of men. All these petitions are addressed to, and can only be met by, our heavenly Father; and the smallest petition is as acceptable to him as the greatest. The one who prays this prayer does so as a child speaking to his father, in an attitude of respectful, trusting submission.

In the sixth chapter of Matthew's Gospel, we are enjoined to be simple in our prayer, because our Father knows all our needs even before we pray to him about them (Mt 6:7-8). However, Jesus does not forbid us to pray and petition God for our needs; indeed, he specifically exhorts us to ask God for all things (Lk 11:9-13; Mt 7:7-11). He also, in two parables, recommends persistence in prayer, to ensure results (Lk 11: 5-8, 18:1-8). We are to approach God in our prayer in a humble manner, acknowledging his greatness and supremacy (Lk 18:9-14). We can always be sure that our prayer is heard and answered (Mk 11:24; Jn 14:13-14; Mt 7:7-11).

Jesus introduces us to the concept that we are children of God, who is our Father. Yahweh was seen as the Father of the community of Israel, but was not, in the Hebrew mentality, seen as a personal Father to individuals within that community. However, Jesus makes it clear that God is a personal Father to us, and that, in this secure relationship, we can pray for anything (Mk 11:22-25). St. John also emphasizes that we are already children of God, through the love that the Father bears for us (1 Jn 3:1).

In the Gospel of John, we are introduced to the concept of praying "in the name" of Jesus (Jn 14:13-14, 15:16, 16:23, 16:26). This is not to suggest that Jesus' name is a magical password, a sort of "open sesame" to receive what we pray for; rather it signifies prayer in accordance with his will, and in his power, as well as invocation of his name. We should remember that, in Hebrew society, to act in the name of someone meant that one represented the person involved and had his full authority vested in oneself. With this concept in mind, it becomes apparent that "to pray in Jesus' name" means that we should pray in that union with Christ which he describes as being the union of branches with the vine (Jn 15:1-11). If we do, indeed, have this union with Christ, through the power of the Holy Spirit and by the will of God the Father, then our prayer will be strong and effective, and we will be joined with Christ as he offers our intercession to the Father.

Now we come to a very important element in Christian intercession: the role of the Holy Spirit as the motivation and guiding force behind our prayer. Christ is himself our chief source of information on this "Paraclete" in the Gospels. In the fourteenth chapter of the Gospel of John, he tells his apostles that he will pray to his Father on their behalf, and that his Father will send "another paraclete" to be with them. The word "paraclete" is frequently used to refer to the Holy Spirit, but it should be noted that Jesus is himself a "paraclete." What exactly does this word mean? The Greek word is variously translated as "advocate," "comforter," "counselor," "helper," "intercessor," "strengthener," or "stand-by." Outside the New Testament, it was used as a legal term, denoting a legal assistant or legally trained person in a court of law; one who pleaded the cause of another. The meaning that most interests us here is "intercessor."

The Spirit will exercise an intercessory function and will remain with the followers of Christ forever. As the Spirit of truth, he will continue to unfold and reveal the riches of the revelation of God to man, and assist Christians in arriving at ever greater depths of understanding of God's Word. It is through the sovereign action of the Holy Spirit in our lives that we will be able to accept and proclaim Jesus as Lord; and only through the indwelling presence of the Spirit in their hearts can men acknowledge God as Father (Gal 4:6; Rom 8:15; 1 Cor 12:3). It is through this understanding and acceptance of the Fatherhood of God that our prayer is completed and concluded, by the power of the Holy Spirit. He comes to our assistance when we, being weak, do not know how to pray or what to pray for, and intercedes on our behalf in prayer too deep for our human language to express adequately. Without the Spirit, our prayer is ineffectual and has no power.

FOUR

Intercession in the Acts of the Apostles and the Epistles

I N THE ACTS OF THE APOSTLES we find several examples of the intercession of individuals and of the community of believers. Very early in the development of the church, Peter and John were arrested by the authorities and warned not to proclaim the resurrection of Jesus. On their release, they and the whole community interceded with the Lord, asking that they might be empowered to continue the spreading of the gospel by word and deed (Acts 4:23-31). Stephen, who became the first martyr of the church, prayed for God to forgive his murderers (Acts 7:60). Simon the magician, after being angrily admonished by Peter for requesting that the apostles sell him the power of which they were the instruments, asks him to intercede with God on his behalf, so that he may escape punishment for his temerity (Acts 8:20-24). When Peter was arrested by Herod, the community of Christians supported him in intercessory prayer (Acts 12:1-5). These and other incidents are reported by Luke in a way that expresses the constant prayer of the Church for her members, and demonstrates the simple, total faith and trust in God which was manifested by her members. Despite this abundance of practical examples, however, there is little theological development of the concept of intercession in the book of Acts.

St. Paul, on the other hand, has a great deal to say about intercession. He bases his teaching on intercessory prayer on the union of the believer with Christ, and the power of the indwelling Holy Spirit. He says that Christians are members of the Body of Christ, joined to him as firmly and inseparably as the limbs and trunk of a human body are joined to the head (Eph 5:30; 1 Cor 12:12-13). In this intimate union with Christ, we are also one spirit with him (1 Cor 6:17). Thus, as Christ is himself the one eternal High Priest and intercessor for all who believe in him, we share in his ministry of intercession, since we partake of his divine nature (2 Pt 1:4), and are coheirs with him, and adopted children of God.

Paul begins most of his letters with prayer for those to whom the letter is addressed. In doing so, he uses a stereotyped formula common to letter-writing of his time, although he alters the content of this formula considerably. Such greetings and prayers are found in Romans 1:8-10, Ephesians 1:16, Philippians 1:3-5, Colossians 1:3, 1 Thessalonians 1:2, 2 Timothy 1:3, and Philemon 4. He often emphasizes an element of thanksgiving in his intercession, thanking God for attributes or deeds of those for whom he prays. This element of thanksgiving should be carefully observed, and incorporated into our own intercessory prayer; all too often we fail to be grateful in our prayer and become merely demanding. In these brief introductory prayers he often mentions that his intercession for the people to whom he is writing is "constant" or "unceasing." In Ephesians 1:16-19, he expands his normally brief mention of prayer to give details of his intercession, asking that God should grant the Christians in Ephesus wisdom, and knowledge of the hope and riches inherent in God's call, as well as understanding of the power that has been given to them through their belief in Jesus Christ.

Paul also expresses prayers for his readers in the body of many of his letters. Among other things, he prays for an increase of love and compassion in the hearts of his readers; asks that they may be made steadfast and unwavering in their faith; invokes the peace of Christ, asking that it may "reign" in their lives; he prays for the salvation of the Jewish people, through their coming to believe in the divine Sonship and messianic role of Jesus Christ; and for greater unity within the fledgling Christian churches; and he asks that God may grant those reading the letters an increase in understanding of what his call to them entails, and that the "fruits of righteousness" may become manifest in their lives. (Relevant texts are Rom 10:1, 15:5-6; Eph 1:16-19, 3:14-19; Phil 1:9-11; Col 1:9-12; 2 Thes 3:5, 16.) He also tells the Colossians that Epaphras, a member of their community who is apparently with Paul, is also interceding in prayer on their behalf (Col 4:12).

Let us now see what St. Paul has to say on the manner in which intercession should be made. He emphasizes our unbreakable unity with God, through the love he has shown us, no matter what obstacles may be placed in our path as we journey towards him (Rom 8:31-39). Because of the intimacy and permanence of our link with Jesus Christ, we have access to the Father (Eph 3:11-12). We are not to be anxious or upset about anything, no matter how great or how small, but are to pray to God for our needs (Phil 4:6 and Col 4:2—note the recurring emphasis on thanksgiving in petition and intercession). Paul further stresses that the Holy Spirit's assistance is indispensable if intercessory prayer, or indeed any prayer whatsoever, is to be effective (Rom 8:26-27).

Paul does not direct Christians to intercede merely for each other, on an individual basis, but also for pagan as well as Christian leaders, and for the whole Body of Christ as well as its individual members. We see that, among other things, he urges Christians to pray for those in authority over them, in order that they as Christians may be allowed to "lead a quiet and peaceable life" (1 Tm 2:1-5). Here, too, the element of thanksgiving in intercession is specifically mentioned, as well as the unique position of Jesus Christ as "the one mediator between God and man." In 1 Corinthians 12:26, we are reminded of our unity within the Body of Christ, and that "if one member suffers, all suffer together; if one member is honored, all rejoice together." This implies a call to intercession for the Body of Christ as a whole, and in Ephesians 6:18, we are again urged to intercede on behalf of all Christians ("all the saints"). We are told to identify with our fellow believers, and to bear with those who are weaker than ourselves, helping them to "carry their burdens" (Rom 12:15, 15:1; Gal 6:2); this assistance naturally involves intercessory prayer, as well as other practical help.

Paul's teaching on our general behavior and attitude as Christians should influence our approach to the ministry of intercession. We are urged to be humble, seeing others as being more important than ourselves, so as to imitate Christ, "who, though he was in the form of God, did not count equality with God a thing to be grasped, but emptied himself, taking the form of a servant, being born in the likeness of men" (Phil 2:3-8). We are advised to teach and instruct one another, and to give praise to God, in order that we may grow in wisdom, and in our unity in the Body of Christ (Col 3:16). Thus, as we grow in holiness and in our understanding of the "mystery of God," our prayer and intercession will become far more effective, being directed more and more in accordance with the will of God, which we will be able to discern more clearly.

In Ephesians 6:18, Paul uses the phrase "pray in the Spirit." This passage has been seen as a reference to praying in tongues by many scripture scholars, both within and outside the charismatic renewal. It is rewarding to view this phrase in the light of 1 Corinthians 14. In verse four, Paul is actually speaking out against an incorrect usage of the gift of tongues in the Corinthian assembly, but in doing so, he says that "he who speaks in a tongue edifies himself." The word "edify" means "to build up" or "to strengthen." In other words, if I pray in tongues, I am "building myself up" or "strengthening myself," in a spiritual sense. Paul says of himself, "I thank God that I speak in tongues more than you all" (1 Cor 14:18). Praying in tongues, therefore, can be seen as a valuable aid to our spiritual growth, as well as an aid to intercession. We should also remember Paul's words on the Spirit aiding our prayer by "interceding for us with sighs too deep for words" (Rom 8:26). However, we should not think that this interpretation ("praying in tongues") of the phrase "praying in the Spirit" is the only one; other interpretations are equally possible. Indeed, many who have experienced moments of deep, silent prayer, of being "face to face with Him Who Is," would agree that such prayer is "praying in the Spirit" in the deepest possible way.

Finally, we should note the many requests Paul makes to his readers for their intercession with God on his behalf, that he may be freed from the dangers that beset him, that his work of preaching the gospel may carry on and bear much fruit, and that God's Word may be triumphant over the forces of evil which oppose it (Rom 15:30-32; 2 Cor 1:11; Phil 1:19; Eph 6:18-20; Col 4:3-4; 1 Thes 5:25; and 2 Thes 3:1-2).

The remaining epistles of the New Testament shed further light on the ministry of intercession. Most of them are short, concise, and scattered, rather than unified or cohesive. As we have already seen, the letter to the Hebrews develops a theological view of Christ as the eternal High Priest, who is always able to grant salvation to those who seek the Father through him, because "he always lives to make intercession of them" (Heb 7:25). That Christ is both priest and victim at the sacrifice means that he both offers our prayers to God and offers himself as a sacrifice to accompany these prayers.

The letter of James contains valuable advice. In illness, the prayer of the elders of the community, made in faith and accompanied by the anointing of the victim with oil, will bring healing (Jas 5:14-16). We are also told that "the prayer of a righteous man has great power in its effects," as in the example of Elijah. He prayed that no rain should fall; and later prayed for rain to relieve the subsequent drought (Jas 5:16-18, referring to 1 Kgs 17:1; 18:1, 41-45; see also Lk 4:25). The phrase "pray in the Spirit" occurs again in the letter of Jude; we are to do this so as to build up our faith (Jude 20).

The first letter of St. Peter reminds us that we are "a chosen race, a royal priesthood, a holy nation, God's own people" (1 Pt 2:9-10). It is with this special calling, relationship, and mission in mind that we carry out our ministry of intercession. In the first letter of St. John, we are assured that we are already the children of God (1 Jn 3:2), which is another encouragement to us in our intercession as we approach our Father. We are also told that if we pray for our brethren when they fall into sin, we can thereby obtain forgiveness from God for their sins (1 Jn 5:16).

The reader should take time to study all scripture passages that I have mentioned. We can never have too great a knowledge of the Word of God, and without this knowledge, our intercession will be seriously impaired. I have not mentioned all possible scripture references in these three chapters, and some of these will come to light in subsequent chapters.

Finally, a passage from the first letter of St. John expresses concisely the guarantees that we have received from God that our prayers of petition and intercession will be heard and answered, so long as they are offered in accordance with his will.

And this is the confidence which we have in him, that if we ask anything according to his will he hears us. And if we know that he hears us in whatever we ask, we know that we have obtained the requests made of him. (1 Jn 5:14-15)

FIVE

The Intercessor

W E HAVE SEEN MANY IMPORTANT facets of the ministry of intercessory prayer developed in the scriptures, which we should take to heart if we wish our prayer to be as effective as possible. But intercession is not merely the learning of these principles, or a repetition of foolproof formulas which, in some magical way, guarantee success. It is rather an inter-action between a human soul and God, between a created being and its Creator. It is an unleashing of power in our human circumstances, and an active seeking of the inter-vention of God's infinite grace into the finite fabric of our human lives. So who, or what, is the intercessor, to seek to "tap in" to the power of God? What are the requirements that this ministry of prayer sets for those who wish to exercise it, and what is the function of the intercessor within the total ministry of the Body of Christ?

The first and most fundamental realization is that the root of all our intercession is in our own personal relationship with God. The stronger our union with God is, and the more we nourish this union through prayer, spiritual reading, and the sacraments, the more we will be led to offer ourselves to him as instruments to be used in the building up of his kingdom on earth. We shall also find that, as our union with God and our offering of ourselves to him grow stronger, we shall be led to offer ourselves as servants to our brethren, for love of God and love of neighbor go hand in hand. Indeed, a personal relationship with Jesus is only possible when we belong to the body of Christ; how can anything or anyone that is not an integral part of the body have any direct link with its Head? If we give our lives to God in a genuine commitment, our prayer will inevitably become more involved with our fellow man, because union with God entails sharing in God's love for all human souls.

Of course, our intercession should be stimulated by the needs of those around us. God is not remote from our human condition; he became incarnate, taking our humanity upon himself. When we see the great needs around us, we should be moved to prayer, inspired by God's vision of our fellow human beings. The Cross has both a vertical and a horizontal dimension, and is not complete in our lives unless both components are present. So, too, our intercession, while made to God on a "vertical" plane, should be inspired by, drawn, from and made on behalf of the "horizontal" dimension of our lives as Christians—the shared anguish and pain of suffering mankind. "No man is an island," and the needs of others are our needs also, since Christ, who lives in us, links us to them through his presence in all creation.

Each Christian has a unique relationship with the Father, through Jesus his Son, in the power of the Holy Spirit, given to us in baptism. In Christ, each of us is a son or daughter of God the Father, placing us in an intimate family relationship with our brothers and sisters before God. We can therefore say that the Christian never prays in isolation, but always as a member of the body of Christ. Our prayer is offered as issuing from, and made on behalf of, the body of Christ, and its results will affect the whole of that body, whether directly or indirectly. As intercessors, we offer to God the needs of people and situations both within and beyond the body of Christ and seek to channel his grace and power to them through our own personal relationship with him, but this relationship needs to be fostered within the unity of Christ's body.

As head of his Body, Jesus offers up a constant stream of intercession for all of his followers. As we are drawn into an ever deeper union with him, we will also find ourselves being drawn into this flow of intercession; our prayers will be joined with his and offered to the Father as one united plea. The ultimate effect of this intercession should be that the entire body of Christ becomes united with its Head to such an extent that their joint prayer is offered with one mind, heart, and voice, whether it be prayer for an individual person or situation, or for something affecting the body as a whole. Even our intercession for people and situations outside the Christian community is offered from within this framework.

What is our function as intercessors within the total ministry of the body of Christ? The intercessor is the arm of the body, supporting the hand as it carries out the various tasks that it is called upon to perform. Any ministry undertaken by the Body of Christ or by individuals or groups within it is in need of support; it cannot function alone. The assistance of prayer is as practical and essential as material support, in order that such undertakings may remain rooted in God, may be carried out in accordance with his will, and may contribute to the building up of his kingdom. Also, the intercessor is needed to spiritually support the body of Christ and its individual members in everyday activities, to provide the prayer support for its continuous renewal of itself, and to act as a channel for God's grace to permeate it and to flow through it to the world.

The intercessor's function of acting as a channel for God's grace is an irrigation system. In such a system, water from a central reservoir or pump is passed through a series of channels and pipelines to reach the growing crops where it is needed. The channels must be laid in an orderly manner so as to get the water to its destination by the shortest and most direct route, and they must be constructed without hollows or gaps, and with a smooth interior surface that will not retard the flow of water.

In the same way, the intercessor acts as a human channel of

prayer, tapping the reservoir of God's infinite grace and directing this power to those people and situations where it is needed. As a channel is laid in accordance with the requirements of its user, so the intercessor's prayer channeling should be directed by God, so that his grace can reach and operate in the needs he desires to meet. The channel does not determine of itself where it wishes to convey the water it contains; the intercessor should not seek to manipulate God to suit his own concept of the needs and situations that require divine intervention and assistance. We are instruments for the Lord to use, not directors and supervisors seeking to control him.

Just as a channel needs to be well constructed, with no gaps or holes that retain part of the water flowing through it or allow the water to escape, and with a smooth interior surface that does not retard the flow of water, so, too, the intercessor must be formed and trained in this ministry. We all, without exception, have "gaps" and "holes" in our lives; these can be habitual sin, unhealed hurts, negative elements in our personalities, or similar things that hamper the passage of God's grace in response to our prayer, and can even block this grace from reaching its desired goal. We also have our normal everyday problems and sins which, while not as serious as these major difficulties, still act as friction, slowing the flow of grace through our lives. We need not despair at these negative elements in our lives, because we do not intercede from our own personal strength, but rather out of the infinite strength and wisdom of God. Rather, we should, with St. Paul, rejoice in our weaknesses, and cast ourselves ever more on the strength and mercy of God, for his grace is sufficient for us, and his power is made perfect in our very weakness (2 Cor 12:9-10). As we grow in our ministry of intercession, we shall find that the Lord seeks to remove and heal these things; we are called to open ourselves to this healing, so that our intercession, in accordance with the will of God, may become more effective.

Yet another analogy illustrates and emphasizes the function

of the intercessor: it is based on the opening line of the Canticle of Mary, "My soul magnifies the Lord" (Lk 1:46). The word *magnify,* means to enlarge, to clarify, to bring out. A magnifying glass, when placed over a page of text and focused correctly, will enable its user to see a word or phrase clearly, enlarging it so that it stands out against the background of surrounding script. In the same way, all Christians are called to "magnify" God in their lives, "focusing" on him to such an extent, so strongly and perfectly, that his presence within them is immediately apparent to those with whom they have contact. This is the most genuine and authentic Christian witness of all; preaching with one's life and example in a way that speaks more effectively than any number of words. However, there is a second implication to the word *magnify,* one applicable in a special way to the intercessor.

Have you ever taken a lens or magnifying glass and focused the rays of the sun through it onto a piece of paper? The paper turns brown, then black, as the concentrated heat acts upon it, smoke appears, and finally the paper bursts into flame. This analogy describes what we as intercessors are called upon to do by focusing the power of God on people and situations through prayer. We do not have any control over his power, and we cannot direct it of ourselves; but we can bring those things for which we intercede within range of this power through our prayers. We should then make ourselves available to God as a "lens" of prayer, through which he can focus his grace onto these things, so that his power is at maximum intensity. As we do this, we shall see the effects of this power, leading ultimately to the pure pentecostal fire of the Holy Spirit burning within the situation that we have brought before God in intercession. As well as magnifying the Lord before the world, we are also called to magnify the world before the Lord, and, through our prayers, offered in accordance with his will, to set it on fire with his love, grace, and peace. We are instruments in the hand of our God: instruments, moreover, whom he asks to cooperate freely with him in the building up and extension of his kingdom. Is there any task that could be more satisfying and fulfilling?

A dirty lens, or one that is poorly ground, is not very efficient at focusing the sun's rays. We cannot expect to be effective "focusers" of God's power from the moment we begin our intercession. It takes time for a lens to be ground out of a piece of glass, and it will take time for God to form us in accordance with his will, so that our intercession may be correct and pleasing in his sight. Just as a dirty lens needs to be washed clean of accumulated grime, so we too need to be cleansed of our sins and faults by the mercy of God before we can operate effectively in this ministry. This is not to suggest that a slightly dirty lens cannot focus light, or that we cannot intercede if there is still sin in our lives (or else no one would ever be able to intercede); but we should be prepared to turn away from this sin, so as to be able to intercede more effectively.

The intercessor, then, should approach life in the conscious realization that he is an instrument in the hand of God, freely cooperating with and subordinated to the divine will, in order to hasten the establishment of the kingdom of God on earth. He should live in the sure hope of God's mercy and the confident realization that nothing is too difficult for God or too insignificant to merit his attention. In that assurance, the intercessor, as a servant and friend, brings before the Lord the needs for which he has been directed to pray, and acts as a channel and focus for God's power and grace to work in and to meet these needs, in accordance with God's will and purpose.

SIX

Effective
Intercessory Prayer

HOW WE SHOULD OFFER OUR PRAYERS of intercession is an extraordinarily complex question. There are almost as many ways of interceding as there are intercessors. It should be noted from the outset that there is no single way of praying that can be considered the best, and none that can be described as the worst. The way in which we offer intercessory prayer will probably be closely linked with the way in which we normally pray. Each intercessor should develop the style and technique of prayer which best suits his personality, situation in life, and spiritual maturity. This chapter will offer some thoughts on the implications of this ministry for the life and attitudes of the intercessor.

Ideally, our prayer should encompass all the diverse elements that we speak of—petition, thanksgiving, intercession, praise, meditation, worship, and so on. However, it is hard to accomplish this unity of prayer when we are praying aloud. Words cannot express half a dozen concepts at once. Many have found that only in silent prayer can they come close to achieving this unity, where praise and adoration are offered simultaneously with intercession.

We have seen that Jesus lived out his ministry of intercession as part of a life of total self-offering to the Father. His most perfect act of self-giving was to willingly accept death on the Cross. He achieved his greatest depth of intercession—when he became the sacrifice that accompanied his prayers—at the moment of his most complete self-offering. Our own intercession should be seen in this light. It only has value when offered in conjunction with the sacrifice and prayer of Jesus Christ: we should constantly seek to follow his self-denying, self-emptying example in order to achieve this. The more we can unite ourselves with his holy act of self-giving, the more we are able to share in Jesus' perfect act of intercession. There are many ways of growing deeper into the mystery of Christ's total emptying of self; personal prayer and the sacraments are only two.

Intercessors generally have come to be involved in this ministry in one of two ways. There are those who are deeply affected by the suffering and need around them, and are moved to pray for divine intervention to remove them. Others, instead of seeking the removal of negative elements, do not question God's purpose in allowing such situations to arise. Instead, they ask his grace and blessing for those who are involved, so that they may persevere in their difficulties, and grow closer to God *through* their adverse circumstances. Both of these approaches have merits; we should use both elements in our own intercession, so that our prayer may be balanced. These two approaches do not contradict each other, despite appearances to the contrary, and both are of use in different circumstances. Whichever way one follows, one should always trust God to do what is right, and not attempt to hold him to a particular course of action.

I would like to consider two elements that are of paramount importance to our intercessory prayer, *humility* and *a listening attitude*. The need for humility in prayer is self-evident in the light of what we have already said about this ministry. We should always be on our guard against coming before the Lord as self-important messengers, bearing news of the needs of his people. He is the Lord and Creator of all: we are his servants, whom he has created. We can, if we are not aware of the danger, develop an overfamiliar attitude towards God. We are, indeed, his friends, brothers, and sisters—Christ himself has assured us of this. But, as well as being our friend and brother, he is also our Lord and King. We should always be aware of his majesty and power, and try to avoid becoming presumptuous and demanding. The old proverb, "familiarity breeds contempt," may sound harsh in this context; but nevertheless it applies. Let a loving respect and an affectionate, devoted obedience be the hallmarks of our intercession. Too often we neglect the Old Testament prophets' injunctions to "fear the Lord your God." Fear, in this context, does not mean terror, but rather a healthy respect for the power of him whom we call "Brother" and "Lord." His power and grace are not matters to be taken lightly.

A listening attitude is necessary for effective intercessory prayer. Our prayer should be offered in accordance with the will of God; if we do not bother to ascertain his will before praying, then we should not be surprised if our intercession seems ineffective. It is all too easy to assume that the solution to the problem for which we intercede is obvious and to pray in accordance with our human feelings. We cannot assume that what we feel about the needs of a particular person or situation corresponds to the Lord's vision. Our prayer cannot be effective if we persist in asking God to follow a course of action that seems good in human terms, but is not the Lord's plan for accomplishing his will.

Experience has shown that the more time spent in the presence of the Lord, seeking his will concerning the object of one's prayers, and listening to him, the more effective subsequent prayer has been. When praying with a group of fellow intercessors, we may spend over an hour seeking God's will, and then, when consensus has been reached about the specific orientation of our prayers, we may take only a few minutes or so for actual intercession. This way of prayer has produced astonishingly effective results.

One may well ask, "How can I be sure that what I sense in 'listening prayer' is, in fact, the voice and the will of God?" There is no sure way for any individual to be certain of this; therefore, group intercession is often better for discernment. However, as the intercessor grows in spiritual maturity and in experience of this ministry, discernment will become easier. Experience cannot be instantly obtained, and there is simply no substitute for it. Real depth in intercessory prayer only comes with several years' experience and a considerable degree of personal spiritual maturity. It can be helpful for those less experienced in intercession and discernment to join a group dedicated to this ministry (preferably one with considerable experience) to assist in developing their discernment and spiritual sensitivity.

Once we are sure of God's will, actual intercessory prayer need not be long-winded. As Christ tells his disciples, "in praying, do not heap up empty phrases" (Mt 6:7). Our heavenly Intercessor, Jesus Christ, is always listening to us, always ready to carry our prayer before his Father, and he already knows the deepest needs of the situation or person for whom we pray. After we have discerned God's will, our prayer should be simple, straightforward, and direct, presenting our need to the Lord and seeking his intervention. Because he always hears our prayers, and has assured us that anything we ask in his name will be granted, we can have faith that our prayers have been heard and will be answered.

We should also bear in mind St. Paul's injunction to "rejoice always, pray constantly, give thanks *in all circumstances,* for this is the will of God in Christ Jesus for you" (1 Thes 5:16-18). Even if we are praying for a particularly bleak situation, we should rejoice in our intercession. We are called to praise God always, even for what appears to be negative elements in our lives. He is able to use these negative factors to produce growth and greater maturity, both in ourselves and in the situation or person for whom we pray.

We can also pray constantly, without fear that we are

nagging God. Once we are praying according to the Lord's will, we can constantly bring our prayer before him. To pray once only, and then forget about it is like a man who fixes a leak in his roof simply by placing a sheet of newsprint over it. He should spend more time and effort making a permanent repair. Otherwise, the next rains will find him with the same problem. In the same way, we should continually bring the object of our supplication before the Lord. Our prayers are like tools in the hands of God, directing his power to where it is most needed. Of course, he could solve all the world's problems instantaneously, if he so chose. But he has chosen to work through human instruments, weak and frail though we are, and to entrust us with the task of directing, through prayer, the power of his Spirit to areas of need.

The Lord seeks not only people of prayer and intercession, but also a people prepared to take active, concrete steps to meet the needs of those for whom they intercede. On more than one occasion I have prayed that the Lord would supply the needs of a particular person or situation, only to hear him say, "I have given you the practical ability and the tools to meet this need, and yet you ask me to meet it in other ways? Go and do something about it!" Intercession is more than a ministry of prayer only. Often it can entail a demanding practical ministry as well, which should not be taken lightly. The Lord can hardly be expected to honor our prayers if we are unwilling to allow him to answer them by using us as instruments of practical help.

We have examined numerous practical aspects of inter-cessory prayer in this chapter, and each of us will have to develop an individual approach to the exercise of this ministry. We each come before God in our own way, and it would be foolish to attempt to prescribe a uniform system of interces-sion. As we grow in spiritual maturity and in our relationship with God, no doubt our way of expressing ourselves in prayer will also become more mature, just as a child's develops with age. The ultimate aim of all our intercession is to touch the mind and heart of God himself: to pray in complete accordance with his will, and to see the results of his power in action.

I should like to close this section with words that all Christians—and particularly all serious intercessors—should carry burned deep into their consciousness. They were spoken by St. John the Baptist after he had baptized the Son of God in the waters of the Jordan. Jesus' example of submissive humility had shaken the saint to the core of his being, and he told his disciples: "He must increase, and I must decrease." If we can make these words the pattern for our lives, and for our prayer, then our intercession will bear much fruit.

SEVEN

The Community of Saints in Intercession

T HE RELATION OF THE SAINTS to intercessory prayer has been the cause of a great deal of controversy among various Christian groups. This chapter will give a brief history of Christian devotion to the saints, as well as a concise explanation of how the Roman Catholic Church sees our relationship to the saints today. I hope that readers of other Christian traditions will also come to a better understanding on this subject.

St. Paul uses the word "saint" to refer to all members of the body of Christ, both living and dead; thus, we are all called to be saints. However, through the centuries since his time, this word has commonly been used to describe those men and women in the body of Christ whom God has used in a special way to accomplish his will in their time. It is with this latter meaning that this chapter will be concerned.

Devotion to the saints arose very early in the history of the Church, during the great persecutions. Those who gave their lives for their faith were revered by their fellow Christians, and even envied. The martyrs were not seen as persons who had left the body of Christ through their death, but rather as those who had entered into Paradise, and into a deeper and fuller life in the heavenly body. It was common for Christians to ask the dead martyrs to intercede for them, just as they would ask one another for prayers. They honored the saints because they had achieved a deeper life within the kingdom—a greater role in the family of God—than was possible on earth. Often, the day of a martyr's death was especially commemorated as the date of the saint's "birth" into the heavenly kingdom.

After Christianity became socially acceptable and martyrdoms ceased, the early ascetics and the great Fathers of the Church who produced an enormous amount of scholarly and theological teachings on the Christian faith came to be held in honor. Many of these "Christian patriarchs," such as Anthony of Egypt, Ambrose of Milan, and Martin of Tours, were later revered as saints, and it was also during this period that the venerable Sts. Augustine and Gregory lived and taught. As the church developed, and came to a fuller realization of the overall implications of Christ's life and teachings, the so-called cult of the saints also grew in importance. Perhaps this is a good place to turn aside for a moment to examine the scriptural foundations of this theology.

Nowhere in the scriptures are we specifically urged to pray through the saints. However, as the scholars of the church studied the Word, they saw that certain of Jesus' promises to the Apostles (for example, Mt 19:28) could be interpreted as indicating that certain people in the next world would be especially privileged. They found, in the parable of the rich man and Lazarus (Lk 16:19-31), support for the concept that those who have died may intercede for the living. However, these theologians' arguments were chiefly based on the wider implications of St. Paul's doctrine of the mystical body of Christ. How, they asked, can it be possible for there to be two bodies of Christ? If we die, we are with Christ, and if we are alive, we live in him; and it therefore follows that the dead remain one with us in the body of Christ, but closer to him, since they have passed the "veil of our humanity," and now see him "as he really is." If this is so, then it is perfectly legitimate to ask them to pray for us and our needs, so that they may aid those of us who are on our way to join them. Theologians consistently emphasized the distinction between the *worship* due to God, and the *honor* and *veneration* due to the saints. At no time was it suggested that the saints were divine in themselves, or that they were able to grant our prayers of and through their own power.

By the later Middle Ages, some popular forms of veneration of the saints had taken on an overtone of actual worship. It was these visible excesses that led many of the leaders of the Protestant Reformation to reject any idea of asking the saints for their prayers. Instead, they emphasized that one could only pray to Jesus Christ, "the one true mediator between God and man." Of course, this statement is correct; but it neglects the principle that we pray with Christ as his brothers, coming before the Father together.

After the Protestant Reformation, when the Catholic Church was engaged in "putting its house in order" and rectifying imbalances in its life, the correct approach to the saints—honor and veneration, not worship—was reemphasized. In the centuries leading up to our own time, this principle has had to be restated and reinforced in order to maintain balance. Catholics have spoken often of "praying *to* Saint So-and-so for help." Many Protestants suppose that this manner of expression implies that the saint concerned actually possesses divine powers of his or her own, and are consequently repelled. Even today, the use of such terms as "praying *to* the saints" still leads to controversy. (I, for one, refuse to use this phrase, preferring to say that I pray *through* the saints, at the same time as I pray *to* God directly.)

In our own time, the Second Vatican Council has restated the reasoning which underlies our devotion to the saints, and to Mary as the foremost of the saints. In the teaching of the Roman Catholic Church, the saints are members of the one body of Christ, as we are. By their lives and works, they have left us an impressive example of what it means to be truly committed to Christ. Because we are in one body with them, we can ask them to pray for us, and for our needs, to the Father, through the Son. They are more closely united with Jesus than we are, because they are now in his heavenly kingdom with him; their prayers are therefore made with greater effect. We may also venerate them for their own example, and may have a personal devotion to them as being living examples of the way in which we should like to conduct our own lives. We are especially encouraged to develop such a devotion to Mary, the mother of Jesus. By her life, she has shown us the most perfect human example of obedience to God, and, through her specially intimate relationship with her Son, her prayers on our behalf carry great weight. She is seen as the mother of the church, and, since we are brothers and sisters of Jesus, as a spiritual mother to every Christian.

Having briefly examined the development and meaning of our devotion to the saints, let us see how we can apply this relationship to the ministry of intercession.

Since we are one body with those who have died in Christ, it is natural and fitting to turn to those in heaven for assistance in our prayers. We would probably have no hesitation in asking a friend or colleague for prayers; why, then, hesitate to ask the prayers of a saint, who is far closer to God than we are? This is of special importance for those occasions when we are interceding alone. Did not Jesus tell us that "wherever two or more are gathered in my name, I am in their midst"? And are we not, with the saints in heaven, "gathered in his name," as members of his body? In this way, our appreciation of praying as a member of, and on behalf of, the body of Christ will be greatly strengthened. I frequently request the prayers of the saints when I am praying alone, so that our joint prayer may be brought before God by Jesus Christ.

In many areas of life, certain saints have been designated by the Church as "patrons" of specific causes or things. (For example, St. Joseph is the patron saint of workers.) The intercessory aid of these saints can be freely invoked in order to sustain and strengthen our own intercession. Another interesting "application" of this approach is that most Christians are named for a saint or saints. Thus, when praying for individual Christians, why not ask their "name-Saint" to intercede for them as well?

I should like to place special emphasis on the importance of Mary, our spiritual mother, in our intercession. Mary is God's masterpiece, his most perfect human creation. She alone was found worthy to give human form to the Son of God. She herself prophesied that "henceforth all generations shall call me blessed, for he who is mighty has done great things for me" (Lk 1:48-49). In her total obedience to God, she is the most perfect example of what we could all become, if we opened ourselves sufficiently to divine grace. Moreover, did not Jesus perform his first miracle—the changing of the water into wine at Cana—at her intercession? At this same event, we see her instructing the servants to "do everything he tells you" (Jn 2:5). What clearer instructions for a dynamic, fruitful, vibrant Christian life could we ask for? In my own prayer life, I initially tended to ignore Mary's importance, dismissing her as having little relevance to the centrality of Jesus Christ, but over the years I have learned that I was wrong. She is now deeply meaningful to me, as my spiritual mother, as a friend in the Lord, and as the paramount example of Christian living. I can only praise God for his wisdom in leaving us so perfect a model of what our human condition can become under the influence of his power.

In this chapter, we have only touched on the importance of the community of the saints in intercession. The reader should obtain and study any further material that comes to hand. To close, I should like to quote from the Second Vatican Council's "Dogmatic Constitution on the Church," *Lumen Gentium,* paragraph 51.

The authentic veneration of the saints does not so much consist in a multiplicity of external acts, but rather in a more intense exercise of our own love, for our own greater good and that of the Church, whereby we seek to learn from the saints "example in their way of life, fellowship in their communion, and the assistance of their intercession." On the other hand, let the faithful be taught that our communion with those in heaven, if it is understood in the full light of faith, does not in any way diminish the worship and adoration given to God the Father, through Christ, in the Spirit; on the contrary, it greatly enriches it.

EIGHT

The Eucharist and Intercessory Prayer

THE EUCHARIST IS ANOTHER SUBJECT on which there is much disagreement among Christian groups. As a Catholic, I believe that the bread and wine in the sacrament are truly and substantially transformed into the body and blood of Jesus Christ. This chapter will discuss the role of the Eucharist in intercession from that point of view. Readers from other Christian backgrounds who differ with this interpretation are asked to approach this chapter with an understanding attitude and to look for common ground.

What does the word "eucharist" mean? It stems from the Greek word *eucharistia*, meaning "thanksgiving" or "to give thanks." The full impact of this word is only apparent when one considers the circumstances under which it was used. At the Last Supper, Jesus was fully aware that he was about to undergo unspeakable torture, and to die a humiliating, lonely death, abandoned by most of his followers. Knowing this, however, he still had the courage to give thanks to God and to share the bread and wine with his apostles, so instituting the greatest of the sacraments. How many of us would be able to show so much courage and dignity at such a time, even knowing that what was about to happen to us would be in accordance with God's will?

The sacrament of the Eucharist is many things at once. It is a sacred meal, the breaking of bread within the community of the faithful. It is a living reality, bringing the presence of Jesus to us in a more powerful way than any other form of prayer. It is a constant reminder to us of his sacrifice on our behalf. It brings us his grace for the forgiveness of our sins, the strengthening of our faith, and the support of our ministry to one another and to the world. It is a sign of the New Covenant, renewing and witnessing to this covenant by reenacting the sacrificial meal at which it was announced. Through it, we offer ourselves to the Father as joint sacrifices with Jesus for the coming of his kingdom. The food and drink of the Eucharist is our spiritual nourishment on the road to eternal life with Christ.

Since in the Eucharist we receive the living flesh and blood of Christ, we achieve our deepest spiritual union with him at the time when we partake of this sacrament. By partaking of his body and blood we become truly one body with him, being lifted out of our sinfulness and into his holy presence. In John's Gospel, Jesus said that we become one with him at this point: "He who eats my flesh and drinks my blood abides in me, and I in him" (Jn 6:56). We are also told that it is because of our sharing in the Eucharist that we have eternal life: "He who eats me will live because of me. . . . he who eats this bread will live forever" (Jn 6:57-58).

With this understanding of the Eucharist in mind, we can appreciate how important this sacrament should be in our intercessory prayer. By linking ourselves in this concrete manner with the sacrifice of Jesus on the Cross, we become one with him in offering ourselves, too, as a living sacrifice, and we share in the glory of his resurrection, communicated to us through the food of his body and blood. In this unity with Christ, our intercession can be presented more effectively and with greater power, than through any other form of prayer.

The events that followed the Last Supper illuminate the effect of the Eucharist in our lives. Jesus was tortured and crucified; his body was broken. In dying, he showed us the depths of his love for and obedience to his Father. It was only after having been broken and killed that he could achieve the glory of his resurrection. Our lives must follow this pattern. It is only by allowing God's grace to break down and eliminate the influences of the world and the evil and sin into which we so frequently lapse, that the life of the resurrected Christ can flourish in our souls. This process continues throughout our entire life on earth. We need to be broken in order for the power of God to make us whole again according to his image.

Is not our intercession for others a plea for God to see their brokenness, their need of healing? Are we not praying for wholeness, new life, and fresh grace in areas of need? In the Eucharist, these prayers can most perfectly be presented to God. We remember the breaking of the Body of his Son, and we offer our needs and the needs of others in conjunction with Jesus' death on the Cross. We hope and trust that, just as Jesus was raised by the power of the Father, so the needs for which we pray will be resolved through the exercise of this same power.

The example of the Eucharist should also influence our view of our own Christian ministry. God loved us so much that he sent his Son to be broken at our hands, so that we might have eternal life. We should expect, if we are sons and daughters of God, that he will likewise offer us to the world as a sacrifice of love. We must allow ourselves to be given, like bread, to feed the millions of people who hunger for spiritual truth. It is never pleasant to be broken, but if we are to proclaim the Gospel by becoming a "living word," we must also proclaim the presence of Jesus by becoming "living Eucharists." We must show forth in our lives the reality of this sacrament, and not be afraid to be broken to feed others; for by our obedience in this, we achieve the glory of the Resurrection.

The intercessor should be available as food for others. Our intercession, as we have seen, calls for us not to intercede as detached observers but to identify with those for whom we pray. In this way, by linking ourselves with them, we become "as bread that is broken." We allow ourselves to feel their needs and to be brought to their level of existence, in order to pray more effectively for them. As they, in their need, are broken and wounded, so we too identify with them in order to intercede from a full realization of their situation. We become a living sign of the New Covenant of love which God has given us, and a living Eucharist to feed those who are dying for want of spiritual food.

We should also remember the meaning of the word "eucharist" and give thanks to God for the privilege of being used as food for others. Christ gave thanks to his Father for choosing him to endure unimaginable agonies of body and spirit in order to bring salvation to all mankind. Our sacrifice will never be as great as his; yet we are always challenged to be thankful for the opportunity to sacrifice our own feelings and desires for the good of others. It is never easy to be thankful for a ministry that can cause us so much pain, but the true intercessor will realize the necessity of self-sacrifice and self-offering by being called upon to do it so often. We must take up the cross of Christ and follow him before we learn the truth about his Cross: that in carrying it, we find true peace, and that its weight, which seems so forbidding and immovable, is within our capabilities, strengthened as we are by God's grace (Heb 13:10-16).

Our prayers are offered on behalf of, and emanating from, the body of Christ as a whole. We have already seen that our ministry is not for ourselves as individuals, but for the whole church. The Eucharist is the focal point of the unity of the church. Sharing in the body and blood of Jesus Christ reaffirms each Christian's unity with the body that is the church. Hence, when we bring our intercession to the table of the Lord, we are offering it in conjunction with all those present, and by their presence they are supporting and affirming our prayer. The burden of intercession is shared throughout the gathering of believers, and our unified prayer is rendered far more effective.

Finally, let us apply the nature of the sacrifice that we proclaim and receive to the call of God on our own lives. As James tells us:

> Be doers of the word, and not hearers only, deceiving yourselves. For if anyone is a hearer of the word and not a doer, he is like a man who observes his natural face in a mirror; for he observes himself and goes away and at once forgets what he was like. But he who looks into the perfect law, the law of liberty, and perseveres, being no hearer that forgets but a doer that acts, he shall be blessed in his doing. (Jas 1:22-25)

We receive both Word and sacrament in our lives. Just as we must allow the Word to govern our actions and form our response to God, so too the Eucharist must shape and form us. In this sacrament, we share in the holy body and blood of Christ. Let us respond by allowing God to use our body and blood as completely as he did the flesh of his Son; and, as intercessors, let us present the needs of his people to God, saying," Lord, this is your broken body; this is your blood being shed. Come in power, and bring the grace of your Son's perfect sacrifice and resurrection to aid us!"

NINE

Intercession in the Life of the Individual Christian

S O FAR, WE HAVE LOOKED at intercessory prayer as a ministry, a commitment to ongoing prayer that we are called into by the Holy Spirit. However, there are many Christians who are not called in this way, for whom offering intercessory prayer can present problems. Some feel they should not be praying like this because it appears selfish or self-centered. Others feel that their level of spiritual maturity is insufficient, or that they are unworthy to intercede, being too plagued by personal problems to pray effectively for others.

In this chapter we shall examine these fears in order to understand the role of intercessory prayer in the life of every Christian. We are all called upon to pray in this way. St. Paul tells us to "have no anxiety about anything, but in everything by prayer and supplication with thanksgiving let your requests be made known to God" (Phil 4:6). It might be argued that this passage really indicates petitionary prayer—prayer offered for one's own needs. However, "one's own needs" can include a variety of problems that at first sight might not be obvious. Our work situation: the government of our country: our church and community: the list is virtually endless. Any disruption in the Christian community to which we belong would certainly affect us; any breakdown in our national government could have serious consequences for the peace and stability of our society. Thus, these "outside" needs are, in fact, our own needs also.

We should also remember our position as members of the earthly body of Christ, the church. We are never called to cut ourselves off from his body: such a way of life is simply not Christianity. Jesus himself pointed out that "as the branch cannot bear fruit by itself, unless it abides in the vine, neither can you, unless you abide in me. I am the vine, you are the branches. He who abides in me, and I in him, he it is that bears much fruit, for apart from me you can do nothing" (Jn 15:4-5). Jesus, on earth, seeks to show himself to the world through his body, the church; in order to proclaim our faith effectively, we should be active members of the church, so that those searching for spiritual truth can look at our fellowship and say, as did observers of the early church, "See how these Christians love one another!" A leaf is still a leaf, whether attached to the branch or not, but a leaf detached from the branch that provides it with food and support will soon wither and die. So, too, we cannot function effectively as Christians unless we are part of a local church community.

Bearing in mind, then, our real need of each other in the body of Christ, we can see that the needs of our brothers and sisters in Christ become our needs also. If a team of men is trying to lift a heavy weight, and some of its members cannot exert their full strength because of some injury or a lack of coordination in their efforts, then that team's work will be severely hampered. In the same way, the mission of the church is made more difficult if her members do not use their potential to the full. In a local church situation, we need to pray that we might not be held back from responding to God's call by immaturity, sin, self-centeredness, or any other reason. In strengthening each other through prayer, we strengthen our local church or community; and because we draw our own support from this body, we also strengthen ourselves. We do not need to have a special ministry of intercession to pray for these needs. On the contrary, we are all called to this kind of intercessory prayer, so that the body of Christ may more perfectly make him known to the world.

In our families, too, there is a great need for mutual prayer support. Wife and husband are called to become "one body, one spirit in Christ"; and this is impossible if we neglect to build one another up through intercession and shared prayer. Our children, too, need constant spiritual support—especially in this day and age, when the social pressures exerted on our young people to turn to immorality and ungodliness are so great. A careful gardener will tie a young sapling to a stake, so that it will not be uprooted or deformed by strong winds. Our children are putting down "roots" into their faith; but until they have acquired sufficient strength and Christian maturity, parental support, and especially prayer, must act as a stake, to hold them upright when the winds of evil blow around them. To be a parent is always a great responsibility, and for ourselves as Christian parents that responsibility is even greater. We should also pray for other Christian families in this regard.

We hear much talk today about "human rights" and "civil liberties." For every right we possess, there is a corresponding duty, and for every liberty granted to us, there is an accompanying responsibility to use it correctly. Evil takes a liberty—such as freedom of speech—and uses it to spread blasphemy, immorality, and falsehood. If we have the right to elect our leaders, we have corresponding duties to pray for them, to use our vote wisely, and to support them in their task. If we have a civil liberty such as freedom of speech, we have a corresponding responsibility to use this freedom in God's service. We have been given certain rights as members of the family of God. Are we also accepting the duties and responsibilities that accompany them? Intercession is one of these duties.

Every Christian should intercede for his or her family, Christian community, and government. There is a risk that, in time, we may come to regard these things as elements in our lives which are not of immediate importance. The forces of evil would like nothing better than to make us forget that these areas directly affect us. Imagine the difficulties that would confront us if we were suddenly deprived of a strong, efficient government, the support of our local body of believers, and a unified family structure. Where would we turn in such a situation? In order to forestall such a possibility, we should be praying constantly for these related areas, that the power of God would sustain and develop them in accordance with his will, and that the forces of evil would not sway them from justice and truth.

Having looked at areas for which every Christian should intercede, we must now ask: how will intercession for others benefit us? What if we feel unworthy or inadequate for such a task?

We are children of God; we have received power through the Holy Spirit and are citizens of God's kingdom. Jesus himself tells us that we shall be capable of works as great as his own, and even greater (Jn 14:12-13). He also assures us, "Whatever you ask in prayer, believe that you receive it, and you will" (Mk 11:24). From these and other sayings of our Lord, we can rest assured that our prayers will never go unheard. God has not merely asked us, but commanded us to bring our needs and the needs of others to him in prayer. We need not hesitate or feel unworthy. We can never achieve "ultimate spiritual maturity" in this life. We are always growing, always learning more about the grace of God, always changing, under the direction and inspiration of the Holy Spirit. We will never be at a peak of spiritual maturity; if we refuse to intercede or to step out in faith until we achieve this peak, we will waste our lives. We should rather accept our limitations, and look to the power of God to transform them through his grace. As the Lord told St. Paul, his grace is made perfect in human weakness; all that we are called to do is to acknowledge our inadequacy and to venture out in faith, trusting in the power of God to implement our prayers (2 Cor 12:7-10).

As we get into a routine of regular intercession for the situations and persons that we encounter, and focus our attention on the needs of others rather than on ourselves, we shall probably begin to change our whole approach to life. To "die to self" is the most difficult task facing any Christian. Intercessory prayer on behalf of others disciplines us to put their needs ahead of our own and to seek God's assistance for them rather than for ourselves. In this way, an awareness of the importance of others is implanted in us, which in turn helps to diminish the influence of pride and self-will in our lives.

The intercessor is a channel for prayer and grace, and for the power of God. A channel conveying water to the place where it is needed is itself cooled and moistened by that same water. In the same way, we will find that our prayers for others serve to open us to God's grace, as well as directing that grace to areas of need.

The foremost practical difficulty affecting people wanting to offer intercessory prayer on a regular basis seems to be finding the necessary time. Many would-be intercessors have complained of having too much to do already, and that they have no free time to use for intercessory prayer. This is nonsense; we can always find time for prayer and intercession. We can pray in the shower, while walking down the street, on breaks from our work. We can add five or ten minutes to our normal prayer time, or use a coffee break at work, pray while driving somewhere, before going to bed at night, during advertising breaks when watching TV—these small amounts of time add up to a substantial total each day.

Many fledgeling intercessors are uncertain about the things for which they should pray. We have seen a number of relevant areas in our discussion, and every reader could make contributions to this list. Some of the more pressing needs could be:

—the ministry of our local church or community, and the guidance of the leadership there;
—the spread of the Gospel of Christ throughout the world;

—peace between nations, and an end to war;

—the problems of nuclear weapons and disarmament;

—prayer for all Christian leaders, that they may lead their followers according to God's will;

—the end of distrust and bitterness between Christian churches, and the healing of the divisions that mar the unity of the body of Christ;

—the continued safety and support of Christians in areas where God's people are oppressed;

—the combatting of evil and pagan influences throughout the world, such as the drug problem, pornography, sexual promiscuity, and crime in general.

There are also the needs encountered in one's own family and professional life. All of these are fitting subjects for prayer and should not be neglected.

There are many different ways in which to pray. One can use words, or remain silent; sing, or pray in tongues. Each person should develop a suitable personal way of prayer. If time is very limited, even a short one-or two-sentence prayer can be offered. God is always present, and will hear the intentions of our hearts even if we don't have time to give him a detailed exposition.

Finally, a word of encouragement: never be afraid to intercede. There are always things needing prayer, and the Lord is always ready to receive our intercession and to take the necessary action. We need not feel inadequate or unworthy to intercede, for he has called us and has made us worthy to stand before him. We do not pray from our human weakness, but from his divine strength and power.

TEN

Intercessory Prayer in Groups

W E NOW EXAMINE ONE OF THE MOST effective approaches to intercessory prayer: to come together with other intercessors to offer prayer jointly. Let us begin with a key passage from scripture, Matthew 18:19-20.

> Again I say to you, if two of you agree on earth about anything they ask, it will be done for them by my Father in heaven. For where two or three are gathered in my name, there am I in the midst of them.

There is a great deal which we can learn from this passage. First of all, when Jesus told us to "agree on earth about anything," he did not mean to imply that if a group of people wished to do something inherently wrong or misguided his Father would assist them to accomplish it. We should remember that "praying in the name of Jesus" means to pray in accordance with the will of Jesus. Therefore, we should agree on something that is in conformity with God's will before requesting it of him in prayer. Discernment is of primary importance here.

Secondly, it is God the Father who acts in answer to our prayer. Jesus is the mediator between God and man; he brings our prayers before his Father, requesting his aid. When a member of a group offers a prayer, Jesus is sitting as part of that group, offering his prayer in spiritual unity with them; and he is simultaneously bringing this prayer before his Father, as the one true and complete intercessor. If our prayer is made in humble, simple faith, the Lord will discern the true intentions of our hearts, even if these are not adequately expressed in our words, and will offer these to his Father.

Let us look at some of the practical advantages of group intercession. Discernment of the correct way to pray is made easier, because everybody can contribute his own interpretation of what God is saying. However, no self-centered or self-interested discernment should become a stumbling block to the unity of the group. If the matter of concern is well-known to the group on a personal level, we can often be led to believe that our own, human ideas on how to resolve the difficulty are what we should ask God for. We should be sure that what we contribute to the group's discernment is not our own instinctive response to a particular issue. While this is difficult at first, a growing spiritual maturity and greater experience in group intercession will provide greater assurance. The group's discernment of the situation should be as much in accordance with the will of God as possible. When this discernment is achieved, it may well be that only a few minutes of actual prayer are needed.

Each member of the group does not pray as an individual, but on behalf of and in the name of the group. Our intercession is offered from our oneness with each other in Christ Jesus. If there are dissensions or divisions within the group or negative attitudes between members of any prayer group they should be brought into the light so that they may be healed. Members of any group should take responsibility to work out any such problems and to be reconciled with one another.

Who should lead an intercessory prayer group? Since the success of the group's intercession hinges on the degree of unanimity which can be achieved through the process of discernment, this unanimity, some feel, obviates the need for a leader. While this approach has its merits, there will undoubtedly be occasions where a decision needs to be made about the discipline of the meeting, or a deciding influence exerted where the group cannot achieve a united discernment. A lack of leadership can be just as dangerous, if not more so, than overly rigid control. Each group must make its own decision in the light of their communal discernment. By its very nature, an intercessory prayer group will usually consist of people with a higher level of personal spiritual maturity than is found in an "ordinary" prayer group. This factor should be taken into consideration when organizing the leadership structure of the group.

Many groups have found it helpful to have a time of repentance before the Lord before proceeding with intercessory prayer, in order to foster a proper attitude of humility and repentance. It is a sound practice to acknowledge our sin to God and to seek his forgiveness. We can also use this time to heal any divisions that have appeared in the group.

The frequency of the group's meetings should be determined by mutual consent. However, once a time and place have been agreed upon, this should represent a binding commitment on the part of each member to be present. The group can only grow and mature in the measure that its members fulfill their commitment to it. Because intercession is a very important personal commitment, the meetings of the group as well as our own individual intercession should have a high priority in our lives. It is also an excellent practice for the members of the group to commit themselves to intercede for each other on a regular basis. Some groups arrange for members who live close together meet more frequently for regular prayer, so as to support and build up each other. Regular intercession by those involved, for each other and for their group, cannot fail to be of great benefit to their joint ministry, as well as for their individual growth.

It has also been found useful for a group to set aside a regular time to pray for itself. During this time, the group seeks specific direction from the Lord as to their orientation in prayer, problems that the members are encountering, and healing and grace for each other.

Many intercessory groups see their ministry as having a general application, and pray for whatever they feel led to. Other groups see their orientation as being more specific: perhaps to pray for a country, or a church body, or a particular section of society. The final answer lies with the joint and prayerful discernment of the group's members. While God often calls intercessory prayer groups into being for a specific purpose, there is also a need for more generally oriented groups. Each intercessory group must discover its own primary reason for existence; this can only be learned from him who has called it into being. Even if a group has a clear and specific orientation in prayer, it should not ignore sudden, extraordinary calls for prayer on subjects falling beyond this area. During the Olympic Games in Munich in 1972, an intercessory prayer group in that city, which saw its primary orientation as being to pray for the conversion of non-Christians attending the Games, received a strong discernment from several of its members that they should pray urgently for the safety of the Israeli competitors. However, because of the predetermined orientation of this group's intercession, this discernment was rejected. Only hours later, Palestinian terrorists attacked the quarters of the Israeli team.

While intercessory groups have many advantages, nothing said here should be taken to mean that intercession on one's own is not as effective as that offered in a group. Many intercessors do not have the time or the ability to join a group; for such people, the community of saints is always at hand. We need never feel alone in our intercession.

ELEVEN

Approaches to Intercession in More Complex Situations

A S WE BECOME MORE INVOLVED in intercessory prayer, we are bound to encounter situations where discernment about how to pray is very difficult. This chapter will examine what we can learn from such situations. The practical examples that follow are drawn from my own experience and from that of intercessory groups.

At the time of writing, and over the past few years, much of Southern Africa has been in the grip of a devastating drought, which has led to a serious shortage of food in many countries. Thousands of people, especially young children, have died from starvation. Since 1980 a group of intercessors scattered all over this region has been praying for relief from this disaster, but we first had to discover how our prayers should be made and to what objectives they should be directed. In the course of our research into the background to this problem, we learned that even if abundant rains were to fall immediately and weather patterns were to remain favorable for the next ten years, this would not be enough. In many regions that there is no seed left to plant, there are too few breeding animals left to rebuild the once-abundant herds, and, due to soil erosion caused by high winds and poor conservation techniques, there is virtually no arable topsoil in which to grow fodder and crops. Prayer for rain was only a part of our problem.

We were staggered to learn that a man, woman, or child dies of starvation somewhere in the world every fifteen seconds. In other words, in the time that you are taking to read this sentence, another person has died through lack of food. This appalling fact does not seem to have generated any adequate response by international relief agencies responsible for help in such situations. These agencies, moreover, have little money; when they can send money, much of it never reaches those who need it, being diverted by corrupt officials in the countries to which it is sent. We saw, therefore, that prayer for international aid alone was also inadequate, and did not address the real needs of the situation.

Such a situation makes the task of spreading the Gospel of Christ virtually impossible. People cannot accept a faith which calls on its followers to share their goods with the needy when those same followers merely pat them condescendingly on the head and say, "Never mind, old chap—God will provide!" While some Christian organizations are rendering superb service and are reaching various needy regions, they are few in number, and their resources are meager.

We went into all these areas, and many more, during our search for discernment as to the way in which we should pray. We felt it our duty to understand the ramifications of the problem as clearly as possible. We needed to respond to this complex problem using factual information, not merely emotional sympathy with those involved. After some weeks of prayer and study, a group of leaders of this intercessory fellowship gathered for a weekend of prayer and fasting, when all the known elements of the situation were examined and submitted to the Lord in prayer. The fruit of this meeting was a list of prayer priorities, which read something like this:

1. Our prayers should be directed at all the elements which contribute to this disastrous situation.

2. The enemy, Satan, is using this situation to his own advantage in many ways; he must be bound and his efforts nullified.

3. We should all be aware that the work of prayer in this situation will be long term, extending through years rather than months. We should pray for each other, so that we may persevere and not become discouraged.

4. Bearing the above points in mind, the main objectives of our prayer should be:

(i) To pray for the governments of affected countries, that they might respond to the best of their ability.

(ii) To pray for the release of funds to international relief agencies, and for the effective application of these funds.

(iii) To pray for all Christians in the drought-stricken areas, that they might share any surplus they have with those less fortunate, and by doing this might witness to the influence of their faith on their lives.

(iv) To pray for Christians in other countries, that they might realize the need of their brothers and sisters here, and give of their relative affluence to share with their fellow-members of Christ's body.

(v) To pray for those who have lost relatives or friends in the drought, that God might use their tragic circumstances to lead them to himself and turn their sorrow into joy.

(vi) To pray for men and women of faith to come and help with the relief work, and so spread their faith by deed rather than by word—a concrete example to those who can no longer accept empty words.

(vii) To pray for rain and the rapid restoration of the soil so that people may soon be able to grow enough to feed themselves once more.

(viii) To pray that God would take all of these negative conditions, in which evil can so easily take root, and use them for the greater glory of his kingdom. In this situation, where man is at his weakest and least powerful, those suffering in the drought are under no illusions as to their desperate need of God.

This example demonstrates the complexity of many problems for which we intercede; to pray "O Lord, bless these suffering people and give them peace!" is not always the most constructive of prayers. Many readers of this book have been or will be faced with problems of similar complexity. In such situations, it is our responsibility as mature Christians and ministers of intercession to investigate the problem in detail and to seek discernment from the Lord as to how our prayers may be most effectively offered. Of course, we can begin praying in general terms while searching for a deeper insight into the problem. We should not use our lack of knowledge, or uncertainty about our discernment, as an excuse for not stepping out in faith to the best of our ability.

As we gain experience of intercessory prayer, we will encounter situations as complex as the one described above. This is not something to fear or to avoid. It is a sign that the Lord is entrusting us with intercessory duties that demand greater responsibility and maturity from us. If we are faithful in our intercession for small, everyday prayer requirements, God will entrust us with progressively more difficult situations, in order to expand our ability to deal with them. In a working career, as we become proficient at one level of responsibility, we will be expected to move into a more demanding position. Jesus used the parable of the talents to illustrate this (Mt 25:14-30; Lk 19:12-27). The servant who had managed his master's affairs wisely was told, "Well done, good servant! Because you have been faithful in a very little, you shall have authority over ten cities" (Lk 19:17). We too can expect to be given greater intercessory responsibilities if we strive to fulfill our present prayer commitments to the best of our ability. We should see this as a sign that the Lord has accepted our commitment to the ministry of intercession and is rewarding our efforts by empowering us to be used more effectively in his service.

When praying for situations that arouse strong emotions,

such as for someone who is dying, we can encounter problems of discernment. Our natural instinct is often to ask the Lord to heal the sick person. However, if that person should not recover after our prayers, but die, we are faced with a spiritual dilemma. "Where did we go wrong?" many ask. Some Christians seem to believe that if someone dies of illness, it is because the deceased or his or her relatives lacked faith. Not only is this heresy of the worst kind, it can have disastrous effects on the already emotionally battered survivors. It would be better to consider death the ultimate form of healing. It might be that it has been God's gracious will to bring his servant home, releasing him from pain and suffering. In many cases, to be sure, the Lord's will is indeed to restore the victim of illness to full health; we have abundant proof of this in his Word. However, nowhere are we told that all illness will be healed in this way. God's ways are not our ways, and his actions are not governed by our expectations.

I've sometimes found it advisable in such situations to pray that all those involved, victim and relatives, should experience healing, without specifying what that healing should be. God can use the death of a loved one to give his peace and light to the survivors, and to lead them to himself. This is also a healing—for them, rather than for the deceased alone. When a close friend of mine died of cancer a few years ago, I was privileged to be at his bedside with his wife. The peace and joy that we felt as his sufferings ended; our awareness that he had gone home, and that we should see him again someday; the powerful presence of God, tempering our natural grief with his peace—all these things beggar description. His death was a victory, not a defeat; a triumph of God's grace, not a tragedy.

Another form of intercessory commitment is to be called to pray for a specific person or group on a regular, ongoing basis. Such a call was the cause of my own involvement with the ministry of intercession. In the early days of my Christian commitment, I regarded intercessory prayer as a minor element of my prayer life. During this formative period I began to correspond with a Christian woman who lived in a city hundreds of miles from my home.

After some months had passed, I sensed a call from the Lord to commit myself to intercession for this person on a daily basis. She was at this time facing several important decisions which would have to be made within the next few years. After consulting with her and seeking the advice of my spiritual director, I began this intercessory commitment. As it progressed, I began to discover just how much was involved in dedicated intercession; in fact, I believe that my prayers for her taught me as much about this ministry as they gave spiritual help to her. On several occasions I sensed something during my intercession and prayed about it (perhaps concerning an event that had taken place in her life, or a direction that she was being called upon to follow) which was later confirmed during our next meeting. As this "intercessory relationship" took root in my life, it was the presence of this "attunement" to intercession which was to lead me into a more general approach to this ministry.

When we sense a call to enter into a committed relationship of intercession, our discernment should be thorough, particularly if it concerns a person close to us. Our emotional reaction to that person may be unbalanced, or there may be an unsound element, not of the Lord, in our feelings towards him. These considerations will not apply to every such situation, but they should be examined. Will our prayers be sufficiently objective and accurate if we are emotionally entangled with the person or situation for whom or for which we intercede? An effective way to counter any such instability is to check out our discernment with our spiritual leaders or directors, and possibly also with the person for whom we feel led to pray. A reluctance to tell anyone in authority over us of our feelings in a situation like this is a sure sign that something is wrong.

Another important element in such prayer relationships is

the depth to which they should be taken. Should our prayer be for the general needs of this person or situation, or should we go into more intimate and explicit detail? In most cases, I feel that we should not attempt to dictate the course of events through our prayer. While we may occasionally receive specific direction from God as to the orientation of our prayers, this should not be seen as the norm for all intercession. The people and events for which we intercede are in God's hands, and it is his overall vision—so much wider and more perceptive than ours—which is best equipped to direct them. During several years of ongoing intercession for the friend whom I mentioned earlier, only on seven occasions have I felt the need to be absolutely specific in my prayer as to what action was necessary. At all other times my prayers have been more general, observing the broad direction in which my sister in Christ was being led, but leaving exact details to the wisdom of God.

Specific calls to intercession on behalf of a particular person or situation are only a part of our ministry. There are many areas of life that are desperately in need of prayer; we should not seek to focus our intercession solely on specific cases to the exclusion of all other needs. Most people, under the guidance of the Holy Spirit, are able to maintain the correct balance in their intercession.

Another aspect of more advanced intercessory commitment is the preplanned intercessory protection organized for a specific outreach or area of activity of the Body of Christ. This can range from a small group of intercessors to a large network of committed persons, spread over a wide area. Many leaders in the body of Christ do not apply effectively the power of prayer available to them in this way. An example of this intercessory prayer protection occurred in an intercessory group with whom I have contact. They were asked to pray for a retreat which was to be held over a weekend and was designed to provide spiritual enrichment and practical training for leaders of several counseling groups. Afterwards, the leaders of the organizing team said that they had never before experienced such a blessed time of retreat, and had been able to get through much more work than usual. They were so impressed by the effectiveness of this prayer covering that they plan to make it a regular element of every such retreat held in the future.

When we encounter any difficult intercessory situation, the basic principles of seeking clear discernment, consultation with those in spiritual authority over us, and seeking the support of more experienced intercessors where necessary still apply. Let us give thanks to God when such situations confront us; a sign that the Lord is seeking to use us in a powerful way as instruments for the building up of his kingdom.

TWELVE

Perseverance in Prayer

HAVING EXAMINED THE CALL to intercession, and the spiritual and practical approaches to this ministry, we will now consider the amount of time we should devote to prayer, and the continuation of prayers over a long period. There is nothing wrong with persistent prayer; we are not going to make God angry by continuing to pray for something that we are concerned about. Jesus himself makes this point very clear in his parables (for example, Lk 18:1-8). Of course, we should be sure that what we pray for is in accordance with God's will. If it is not, we will get no result for our efforts. In fact, if we are persistent in our prayer, we shall find that the passage of time allows our initial discernment to be tested and refined, so that our prayer becomes more accurate.

How should we approach persistent prayer? We've seen that our actual prayer should not be pompous and long-winded. We should be brief and to the point, as the process of discernment shows us the exact needs to pray for. This short, concentrated prayer can be held in our minds for months or even years. We can turn to the Lord in free moments of our time and lift up the needs of the person or situation that we are concerned with to the light of his presence in our lives. We can pray in silence or aloud, in tongues or in our own language, in public or in private—the possibilities are endless. We have a God who has promised that he is always with us, no matter where we are or what we are doing. It is in the assurance of this constant presence that we persevere in intercessory prayer.

The fruit of the Spirit, patience and longsuffering, come into play here as well. Because actively interceding for something or someone for many months without seeing any results can be very frustrating, we may fall victim to the temptation to abandon our intercession, in the belief that our efforts have been fruitless. Worse still, we may begin to feel that our initial discernment was wrong and that we should never have been praying for this subject in the first place. Therefore, if we feel that we should begin to intercede for some particular situation, and that this intercession will be prolonged, then our discernment should be all the more careful and thorough. Once God has issued a call to intercession for something or someone, only he may retract or end that call. I have encountered situations where the person for whom a group has been praying has asked them to cease their intercession, as it seemed to be unnecessary; subsequent events have proved that further intercession was, in fact, vitally necessary.

There are groups and individuals engaged in the ministry of intercession whose activities are almost entirely devoted to ongoing, persistent prayer for problems facing nations or people and groups within society. In my own country, South Africa, there are many such groups. We have vast and complex problems here, with an entrenched system of racial prejudice and intolerance, which have frequently erupted into violence and bloodshed in the past. To counteract this, there are many groups, as well as a network of committed individual intercessors, who have pledged themselves to regular intercession for the needs and problems of our country. Other long-term commitments include prayer for a particular outreach or ministry of the body of Christ, or for the needs of specific professions, groups, or individuals.

In such situations, the focus of prayer often changes from time to time. As new events take place and affect the areas for which we pray, so our prayer should also expand to include these more immediate needs, as well as maintain a forward-looking, longer-term view of the situation. In this way, our intercession for events of the present can be integrated into the greater, more permanent work that the Lord seeks to accomplish in the situation. Our discernment of the Lord's ultimate intentions can also help us to see how these events fit into the Lord's will, and to pray and act accordingly.

Perseverance in intercession is also of great value for our own spiritual growth. Most Christians experience cycles of dryness and aloneness in their walk with God. The negative effects of these times can be greatly reduced if we have acquired the habit of regular, committed prayer, not only intercession, but also more general personal and liturgical prayer, and persevere in it. Even though we do not have the same awareness of the presence of the Lord, he honors our faithfulness to him in prayer and will continue to guide our intercession and to act in response to it. Anyone can pray, and enjoy it, at times when the presence of God is immediately apparent. It takes determination and real commitment to do this in the spiritual deserts through which we must all pass. When we fall down on our responsibilities here, it can be a very painful thing to realize that we have so little faith and perseverance. However, if we continually try to remain faithful to our commitment to Christ, and in our intercession, God's grace will aid us in our weakness, and we shall grow ever deeper into him.

Many intercessors have found it valuable to keep a "prayer diary." This describes their day-to-day intercession; what they have prayed about, details of their discernment about it, the specific orientation of their prayers, and similar details. They also record details of how the Lord has answered their intercession. As time goes by, this record of prayers made and answered will become a valuable resource for further prayer.

Not only does it strengthen our faith to see how God has moved in answer to our prayers in the past, but we can also see where his action has differed from our discernment of what was required. In this way, we can continually check our discernment, and correct it.

This diary of prayer is also a valuable aid to other intercessors. While one should not make it freely available to anyone, in a group of intercessors who are committed to mutual support, it is very useful to be able to learn from the recorded experience of others. To guide another person past pitfalls that we have encountered is a valuable service. We can also be corrected by others from their experience. It takes courage to expose the weaker elements of one's prayer life to others, but we are told that all things should be brought into the light, so that the darkness of concealment cannot confuse or cloud the issue at stake (Jn 3:20-21; Eph 5:8-13). This sharing of experiences between committed intercessors has great value.

We should also persevere with our own prayer and spiritual reading, and continually seek to develop and deepen our personal relationship with God. The longer we spend with someone, the more we are able to understand him; our relationship with our Father in heaven works in the same way. We can only receive from a relationship what we are prepared to put into it. Moreover, we should try to avoid personal sin. Water can't flow through a blocked channel; unconfessed or habitual sin in our lives will certainly hamper the effectiveness of our intercession.

There have been many great intercessors in history, and also in our own times. These men and women have frequently written of their experiences, or have had others write about them. While prayer is very much an individual matter between oneself and God, such material is of inestimable value in helping us to develop our own approach to intercessory prayer. We can incorporate the lessons that others have learned into our own method of praying, and so avoid many pitfalls. The reader will no doubt encounter many such figures from the past and present. Three that I should particularly like to recommend for further attention are St. Therese of Lisieux, Andrew Murray, and Rees Howell.

Ultimately, the effectiveness of our intercession must depend on the measure to which we are willing to commit our lives to God. Just as practice and dedication are necessary to become proficient in any task, so our Christian lives must be sincere and complete if we want to see our intercession bearing a rich harvest of grace. We should always seek to grow deeper into the mystery of God's love, and to unite ourselves with the mission of salvation of his Son. If we are determined to follow his example, then he will supply the grace we need to maintain our living witness, and to present an inspired, intercessory example to the world.

THIRTEEN

Intercession
and Discernment

O F ALL THE SPIRITUAL "TOOLS" given to us to help in this
ministry, the gift of discernment is perhaps the most
vital. In human terms, "to discern" means "to perceive" or "to
realize." In other words, we discern (or perceive) a reality that
had previously been unknown to us, or which we had not
clearly understood. Discernment is the process of acquiring
knowledge or certainty about something. In spiritual terms,
this same understanding applies—except, of course, that it
refers to spiritual as well as temporal realities.

The intercessor needs to "touch the mind and heart of God"
in prayer, and to pray "in the name of Jesus," that is, in full
accordance with his will. We can come to know God's will by
getting to know him personally through prayer, by progressively allowing his Spirit to empty us of everything that blocks
our spiritual lines of communication, and by studying his
Word and learning from the lives of those who served him in
the past. The primary requirement for discernment is a life
geared to God's will, seeking to grow in faith and in
knowledge of his ways.

Our prayer life should be constant and ever-deepening. It is
our communication with God, and discernment is difficult
unless our search for truth and right judgment is rooted in a

sound prayer life. To use a human analogy, intimate acquaint-ance in marriage comes about by regular, far-ranging conver-sation, and by living together continually. It is only through a life lived in the constant awareness of, and response to, the presence of God that the intercessor can come to know him well enough to discern his will with unfailing accuracy. Of course, this takes time, but God's grace will always show us the direction and guidance we seek in time of need, and help us to grow in our understanding and experience of discernment.

When I first became involved in the ministry of intercession, I made errors of discernment. My problem was pride: I was overconfident of my ability to judge situations and needs. Since God had given me his Holy Spirit, I reasoned, I could not possibly go wrong. My judgment of a situation would certainly be God's as well. My fellow intercessors had to correct my over-enthusiasm and recklessness. This problem is a common one for beginners in the ministry of intercession, and clearly demonstrates the need for an importance of group discernment which acts as a safeguard against individual error.

Despite our worries about accuracy of discernment, how-ever, we need not be afraid to step out in faith and seek God's will. If we look to his Spirit for guidance, he will give it. The Lord has shown us his will through the situations he encountered in his earthly life, and we can learn from his example. God's Word in scripture also gives us clear teaching to guide our discernment.

When we begin to seek discernment of God's will, the assistance and advice of more experienced intercessors is invaluable. This is where intercessory groups can provide a vital service. They offer a training ground for newcomers to intercession, where they can be helped to develop their capabilities and to become more sensitive to the demands of this ministry. With greater experience, the intercessor is better fitted to launch out into greater depths of personal interces-sory prayer, without the need for so much group feedback. However, if no intercessory fellowship is available, we need not fear to seek guidance from God. He has promised us that our call for help will not go unanswered.

It has often been found in group intercession that each member has an element of the overall discernment that is needed. Only when all have contributed their share does the pattern become clear. Consensus is important, because if a group is united in its discernment, their subsequent prayer will be strengthened by their agreement over the manner in which to pray.

Discernment can and should come, at times, from others who are not committed to intercession as a ministry. On occasion, Christians whose spiritual authority and maturity we acknowledge may ask us to pray for a particular situation in accordance with specific discernment that they have received. We should, of course, act responsibly when considering such discernment; we should pray about the request, seeking to confirm the discernment given to us. In accepting such requests, especially from such figures as our shepherds and pastors, with whom we have frequent dealings, or from leaders in our local Christian communities, we are working for the greater good of the body of Christ.

Discernment not only tells us when and how to pray, but also when to stop praying—and, indeed, when we should not pray at all. Jeremiah was forbidden to intercede for Israel by the Lord, because the people would not leave their sinfulness and mend their ways (Jer 14:11-12). In the same way, there are situations today where our intercession cannot be effective, because those for whom we pray are not interested in responding to God's grace. When such unfortunate situations do arise, we should be able to discern the problem and react accordingly.

We should also use our spiritual discernment to seek the Lord's direction as to when our intercession should cease. If our prayers have been answered, and the Lord has taken action in response to our requests, we need not continue to nag him. The difficulty here is that God might have answered our prayers in a different way from that which we expected. When this happens, our own expectations can blind us, preventing us from seeing what he has done. Correct discernment of God's will should correct this imbalance.

We hear the Lord in our own individual and unique ways. Some may hear God clearly in their minds, almost as if he were actually speaking aloud. Others sense a less definite communication, best described as an inner conviction or feeling about what must be done. Many have said that they turn to the scriptures for answers to problems of discernment, seeking a passage that describes situations akin to those they are praying for, and then seeing what the biblical answer to that particular problem has been. Still others feel that their answers come through the normal everyday events of their lives: they relate these to the persons or situations for which they pray. No one method of discernment is complete in itself; each complements the others. It seems best to attempt to integrate all of these ways of discernment within our own intercessory ministry. A group of intercessors can be more confident of their joint discernment, because each member uses his own approach to contribute to the overall consensus of opinion.

We should not pray about any important subject without first having sought to gain as accurate a discernment as possible of God's will concerning it. If things are urgent, we simply don't have time to seek detailed discernment. In these situations, the most effective way of prayer is to offer the entire affair to the Lord without making specific requests as to the action he should take. If we have no clear discernment, we can trust in the mercy of God who knows the intentions of our hearts, and simply pray as best we can.

As we grow in spiritual maturity, and as our overall prayer life continues to deepen, we draw closer to God, and discernment of his will is easier. But what happens in the dry times, those spiritual deserts through which we all pass? We can rely on what we have learned about God's will in the past to tide us over our present dryness. If we are really unsure what his will might be in a particular situation, we can use our common sense and apply the general standards that he has given us. We can often make our prayers in a more general sense, recognizing and applying the principles of Christian life that have been revealed to us. If the "desert" is really hot and dry, I simply commit my prayer to the Lord before I make it, and pray in silence or in the Spirit. The Lord, who knows all that is in our hearts, will supply what our human weakness cannot.

As many intercessors gain experience in the exercise of discernment, they are used more frequently for the so-called "word gifts"—prophecy, words of knowledge, and the like. This is to be expected. A continuing effort to attune oneself to God's presence so as to discern his purpose for the object of one's intercession will almost invariably produce the additional benefit of a greater awareness of the Lord in other situations as well. In addition, we should remember the Old Testament understanding of intercession as a major responsibility of genuine prophets.

Finally, we should remember that the Lord has not called us into the ministry of intercession without equipping us with the necessary tools to do the job. Discernment is one of the most important. We will not be left in darkness if we are genuinely seeking the Light. As long as we are sincerely trying to grow closer to the Lord, and to empty ourselves of self-will and pride, we can trust him to provide the spiritual power and grace to complete the job. As St. Paul points out (2 Cor 12:9-10), God's strength is made perfect in our weakness.

FOURTEEN

Spiritual Warfare
and Intercession

IN APPROACHING SPIRITUAL WARFARE, the most important
thing to remember is that we cannot be defeated if we
remain rooted in and directed by the will of God. Where the
Holy Spirit is, no other spirit can be. Our first priority is to
walk in the light of God's presence, and to be faithful to him in
our prayer and in our way of life. Many passages of scripture
(especially Gal 5:16-26; Eph 6:10-18; Jas 1:12-16, 4:7; 1 Pt
5:6-11; and 1 Jn 1:5-10) discuss our conflict with the forces of
evil, and our own conduct as children of the Father when
confronted with Satan's works.

The first way Satan tries to disrupt our intercession is by
attacking us with temptations to sin, and by trying to make us
focus on the negative elements in our lives. When we do sin,
rather than indulging in our feelings of guilt and the subtle
condemnation of the devil we should repent and seek God's
forgiveness. St. John writes:

If anyone does sin, we have an advocate with the Father,
Jesus Christ the righteous; and he is the expiation for our
sins, and not for ours only but also for the sins of the whole
world. (1 Jn 2:1-2)

Our Lord Jesus died so that our sins might be forgiven; our Father longs to pardon us our sins and receive us back into his love. The powerful help of the Holy Spirit, the Paraclete, is always with us. It is in his strength that we are able to resist temptation and refute Satan's empty allegations of guilt.

One of the devil's favorite tricks is to try to focus our attention on the evil and negative elements in the things we pray for. When we see the effects of evil in a given situation, we often react by praying only against this evil to the exclusion of the other problems facing us. There are, of course, times when direct action against evil is necessary; but we should not overemphasize the role played by the forces of evil. Let us rather focus our attention on God's presence, and bring his light to bear on the situation. Where light is, darkness cannot be. In this way, the forces of evil are removed without giving them undue prominence, and all glory is God's. We should not give so much attention to the activities of Satan that the victory won over him by our Savior seems to take a second place.

Sometimes it is necessary to confront the forces of evil directly. If we are walking in the light of Christ and are armed with the sword of his Word, the powers of darkness cannot harm us and must yield. However, we must take certain basic precautions. We should not attempt spiritual combat of this nature if we are ourselves in a state of major unconfessed sin or moral laxity. We cannot expect to bring the light of Christ to bear on Satan's works if the darkness of sin in our own lives prevents us from functioning as fully effective instruments of the Holy Spirit. Direct action against the enemy is best undertaken as part of an intercessory group. The strength and discernment provided by the spiritual unity of the group will be far greater than an individual intercessor's.

While studying in Pretoria, South Africa, in 1979, I became involved with an intercessory group there. One of our members became aware of a problem among the young people of a suburb of the city. Several incidents of drug abuse had been reported, and there were rumors of Satan-worship that disquieted us. After praying about the situation together and seeking discernment for some weeks, we felt that direct action was necessary. Accordingly, we spent an afternoon praying against the activities of the persons and evil influences behind these problems, and maintained this prayer offensive for about two weeks. Shortly after we began to pray, the persons concerned simply vanished from Pretoria and were not seen there again. All of us experienced spiritual counterattacks in the form of temptations to sin, depression, and similar problems, but because we were united in discernment and purpose, we had no real difficulty in coping with them.

The devil also attempts to disrupt our intercession by activity against the person or situation that we are praying for. A good example would be an effort by a Christian group to lead alcoholics to healing through commitment of their lives to God. To frustrate such an outreach, Satan can be expected to attack the persons involved with temptations to return to their drunken way of life, or to weigh them down with feelings of personal guilt. We need to anticipate such a reaction to our prayers for such a ministry, and to forestall the devil by invoking the protection and power of the Holy Spirit before the enemy has a chance to make mischief. We wield the power of Jesus Christ as our primary weapon in this spiritual combat. Satan may try all the tricks he knows to evade that power, but he cannot ultimately escape it. We stand firm on the reality of our relationship with God and the presence of the Holy Spirit in our lives.

The drastic moral decline in our society demonstrates how powerfully the forces of evil are attacking our spiritual and temporal values. In many nations today abortion is legalized, pornography is freely available, and immorality and permissiveness are the order of the day. Our leaders need prayer support, so that they may be influenced and strengthened to stand firm against such evil tendencies in society and be given the courage to take action where the effects of Satan's work are apparent. Because this evil onslaught must be fought on both worldly and spiritual levels, we should pray for all those involved in the struggle: the politicians, judges, police, and education authorities as well as church leaders.

An important element in our resistance to the devil is our own outlook on life. To use an analogy, when we look at a grey, cloudy sky and think dismally of the bad weather in store, we don't remember the glorious, sunny day we experienced yesterday, or think of the fine weather that will surely return. Still less do we remember that above the clouds, the sun is shining brightly. This preoccupation with present miseries is what Satan tries to induce in us. He seeks to bring the knowledge of our sinful nature, and our spiritual difficulties, between ourselves and God, so that when we look for the Lord we only see our problems. We should remember that on a cloudy day, we have only to fly up through the clouds to emerge into brilliant sunshine. In the same way, we have only to step out in faith, looking to the grace of God rather than our own shortcomings, to be relieved of our burden of doubt, and for Satan's attack to fail. The light of God never fades; his power is always at hand to help us combat the tricks of the devil. To quote St. John once more, "If we walk in the light, as he is in the light, ... the blood of Jesus his Son cleanses us from all sin" (1 Jn 1:7).

One of the most effective weapons in Satan's arsenal is to convince people that he does not exist. All over the world, wherever there are problems like malnutrition, famine, slum conditions, or the exploitation of labor, we hear incessant arguments about the causes of the problem. It is blamed on the greed of capitalists, the lack of adequate facilities, big-power rivalry; but in every such situation, the enemy is at work. It is his influence that makes man greedy and uncaring for his brother's welfare, his influence that makes us slow to give help to others, his influence that motivates those who lord it over the poor. While we should continue to pray for relief of these problems, we should also come against the work of Satan by praying for light in the sin-darkened hearts of those directly responsible for such conditions. If we bring the light of God into the situation, that light will expose and do away with the works of darkness.

We should also consider the implications of intercession when this ministry is linked to that of deliverance or exorcism. We should be cautious in our approach when such problems are suspected, and seek clear discernment. Genuine cases of possession by an evil spirit are seldom encountered in Western society. We are all subject to spiritual oppression such as attacks against us in the form of temptations to sin, but this is a far less serious problem than possession. The discernment of a genuine case of possession is best left to those who have experience in this ministry, and have been recognized by their brethren as being competent in such situations and authorized to deal with them. While the ministry of deliverance has its own specialized requirements, gifts, and abilities, intercessors play a very important supporting role by providing prayer support for those involved, especially shielding them from spiritual counterattack by the devil.

Many intercessors begin all prayer by invoking the protection of the Holy Spirit and binding Satan from interfering. This is a worthwhile precaution and can prevent many problems at a later stage.

Finally, we must remember that the forces of evil have been defeated once and for all by the sacrifice and resurrection of our Lord. We need not treat them as formidable, unconquerable opponents; they are already a beaten force, despite their pretense to the contrary. Let us focus our prayers ever more closely on the Lord and seek to implement his will through our intercession. As our prayers direct his light into the darkness of the world's problems, the forces of darkness must inevitably make way. Let our concern be for him who is our light, Jesus Christ.

FIFTEEN

Fasting
and Intercession

FASTING AS AN ACCOMPANIMENT to prayer seems to have lost favor with many people today; yet only a few years ago, it was a compulsory discipline for millions of Christians. We have come to ignore the real benefits, both spiritual and physical, that fasting can provide as a "self-centered society" has grown up. Secular patterns of thought have led us to put our own physical comfort and satisfaction before everything else.

Fasting can be of assistance in many areas of spiritual activity, such as during retreats, as an aid to many forms of prayer, as an expression of repentance and humility, and so on. It's not my intention to suggest that intercession is deficient or less effective if it is not accompanied by fasting. This chapter will examine fasting in the scriptures and provide some practical advice for those who are beginning to fast as an aid to spiritual self-discipline and intercession for others.

There was only one obligatory fast in the Jewish calendar, on the Day of Atonement (Lv 16:29-30; Nm 29:7). Nevertheless, the Old Testament shows us that fasting was a very widespread practice. A fast was undertaken either for one's own purposes, or because it had been officially decreed for some reason. The duration of fasts varied between one day and two weeks. It appears that most Israelite fasts involved complete abstinence from food, but, except in certain special cases one could drink water.

Fasting was used as a ceremonial form of penance at public worship (Jgs 20:26; 1 Sm 7:6); as a preparation to receive God's revelation (Ex 34:28; Dn 9:3); to show sorrow for having sinned (1 Sm 7:6; Sir 34:26); to avert God's punishment for wrongdoing (1 Kgs 21:27) or to appease his anger (Jl 2:12-17). Fasting also accompanied petitionary and intercessory prayer (see, for example, 1 Sm 14:24; 2 Sm 12:15-23; Ezr 8:21; and Jl 1:14, 2:12-15). Fasting, in Old Testament practice, was an attempt of the person involved to humble his body as an external sign of the spiritual sign of the humility he felt. It was an attempt to move God to pity by self-imposed physical deprivation. Fasting was seen as a prayer in itself, which was accompanied by, and completed in, the spoken prayer; it hoped for all things from God (see Is 58:3), and was seen as a method of prayer which guaranteed results.

After the return of the Jews from the Great Exile, fasts were undertaken four times during the year to remind the people of the sufferings they had endured (Zec 7:3-5, 8:19). As the Pharisees developed a more rigid code of religious practice, fasting became very common as a personal act of devotion, and was highly regarded. In time, this developed into an ostentatious show of humility and holiness, against which Jesus was to warn his disciples. It would seem that many Pharisees ignored the spiritual reality underlying the practice of fasting, and the act became a purely outward ritual.

Jesus never spoke against fasting as a practice, but rather against this superficial, pride-filled external rite. He stressed that humility, not demanding pride, should be our attitude (Mt 6:16-18). When legalistic Jews wanted to know why his disciples did not fast when the Pharisees and the followers of John the Baptist did, he explained that fasting was inappropriate to times of joy. His presence was a source of such joy to his followers that they did not need to fast. When he had gone, there would be time enough for fasting (Mt 9:14-15). He himself fasted for forty days after his baptism (Mt 4:2), before commencing his active ministry. He specifically links prayer and fasting as a means of exorcism (Mk 9:29). Jesus teaches that fasting is a worthwhile and effective practice when undertaken in a spirit of humility and submission to God. He reasserts the spiritual reality underlying the physical practice.

The rest of the New Testament does not teach about fasting, but gives practical examples. When Paul and Barnabas were sent out, the elders of the community at Antioch fasted and prayed (Acts 13:2-3). They were already engaged in fasting when the Holy Spirit was heard; they used fasting with prayer to prepare themselves to hear the word of God. Paul and Barnabas also prayed and fasted when appointing elders of newly established Christian groups (Acts 14:23). Another text that I have found helpful is 1 Peter 2:11. Although the apostle is not talking specifically about fasting in this passage, his point remains valid in this context. By fasting, we can establish an inner discipline over the "passions of the flesh" and so subordinate our bodies to our will.

Our approach to fasting should follow these scriptural guidelines. We fast in order to express, in a physical human way, our complete identification with the needs for which we intercede. Fasting is not a magical action which, like the waving of a wand, will produce supernatural results; rather we see it as something which is performed simultaneously with the offering of our prayers. It helps us to concentrate our attention on God and on that for which we pray.

Fasting can provide great physical benefit as well. Those of us in Western culture eat so much "junk" food, and abuse our bodies to such an extent, that a period of abstinence allows our natural functions to cleanse our system of accumulated impurities. This cleansing process can produce temporarily unpleasant side-effects, such as headaches or stomach cramps. If these are severe, or do not pass away after a time, the fast should be discontinued and a doctor consulted. People with physical disorders such as diabetes or low blood pressure should not fast without medical approval. Anyone who is in doubt about whether he can fast safely should consult a doctor.

When beginning to fast for the first time, one should take care not to overdo things. Although Moses, by God's special providence, may have been able to go without food or drink for forty days, we should regard this as an exceptional calling, and not the norm. It is better to start with a short fast, perhaps for a day only. As one grows accustomed to the experience, the duration of the fast can be extended. Many experienced intercessors feel that any fast longer than a day should be undertaken under the supervision of a spiritual director. We should take account of the physical demands on us during and immediately after the fast. If strenuous physical activity becomes necessary then the fast should be shortened, or a little food taken in time to regain strength before the work. This may present unpleasant physical repercussions such as nausea, dizziness, and vomiting, or long-term damage to our health due to over-exertion.

It is also important to continue to drink liquids while fasting, as dehydration is an extremely dangerous condition. Liquids also keep one's bodily functions active, diminishing or preventing unpleasant conditions such as constipation. (It should be remembered that, in longer fasts, constipation is inevitable; if one is taking no food in, the body has no waste products to get rid of.) After a fast of longer than a day or two, one should take care not to eat too much too soon. The stomach shrinks when not in use for a time, and severe indigestion will result if it is suddenly crammed to the bursting point. The longer one's fast has been, the longer should be the recovery period of light eating. Self-discipline is needed here, especially when, after one's stomach begins to return to normal, one's desire for food suddenly increases. The sort of food one eats is also important. Since the body has been purifying the organs and bloodstream of accumulated impurities during the fast, it doesn't make sense to eat non-nutritious foods immediately after the fast is over. I have found that lots of salads and green vegetables act as an internal cleansing agent after a fast, providing food and also, through their laxative effect, completing the process of removing impurities.

We need not fast for everything we pray about. Such a practice is not seen in the scriptures—and besides, if we were to fast for every prayer we make, we would soon be permanently beyond any further need for earthly food. Fasting should be reserved for issues that are of real importance. If we practice it too freely, we run the risk of becoming offhand about it. When we do fast, we should use the time as productively as possible. Because we cannot always take time off from our normal activities to conduct our fast, we may not have much extra time for prayer. The time that we would normally spend eating can be profitably used for prayer, spiritual reading, and meditation. Where a group of intercessors are undertaking a fast together, the group might meet during free mealtimes or on other occasions for joint prayer.

In one group in South Africa, I encountered "relay fasting." When I took part in one such fast with this group, I found it not only of spiritual benefit, but great fun as well. It worked like this. Our group had been asked to pray for a mission team for a period of two months while they were engaged on a specific outreach. After joint discernment, we felt called to fast as well; but how were we to do this for so long a period? Eventually we hit on a practical solution. We divided ourselves into five teams of two persons each; each team fasted in turn for two days, being relieved at the end of that period by the next team. Our prayers were answered, and the ministry of the mission team bore much fruit. Moreover, a good time seems to have been had by all concerned. We are not called to be miserable when fasting, even for prolonged periods; there is nothing wrong with finding enjoyment and pleasure in one's fast.

A final word of warning about fasting. It is spiritually unhealthy to set ourselves targets which are too high, especially when we are unused to fasting. It is better to start with short periods and to work up to longer fasts over a period of several months. We may well become discouraged if our bodies can't adjust to a prolonged fast at the first attempt; and the devil will try to use our negative feelings to induce us to break our fast, or to abandon future attempts. Be on guard against him! We can expect increased spiritual attacks against us while fasting; since we and those for whom we pray can derive such great spiritual benefits from it, it is only logical to expect the enemy to try to deny us the fruits of our efforts. As long as our motivation is correct, and we remain constant in prayer and intercession during our fast, we need not fear.

Many intercessors and intercessory groups all over the world observe a fast on the first Friday of every month, as a regular discipline and a joint prayer effort. I would like to suggest that we all begin to participate in this fast, if we are not already doing so, and thus present a worldwide intercessory plea to the Lord on a regular basis. One day a month is not very much to ask, and the spiritual benefits derived from being a part of such a large group effort could be very great. In this way, and through our own fasting, our intercession will become more effective.

SIXTEEN

The Repentant Intercessor

A PERSONAL UNDERSTANDING of our need for repentance before God, before our brothers and sisters, is indispensable if we are to become mature, effective intercessors. Christian teachers and spiritual leaders have constantly emphasized that we cannot develop spiritual maturity without turning away from sin and dedicating ourselves to godly lives. If this applies to all Christians, how much more necessary to intercessors, who seek to aid and strengthen others through their prayers. It is no use throwing a rope to a drowning man if the rope is too short to reach him or too weak to bear his weight. If we are to provide spiritual support to our brothers and sisters, let us cleanse ourselves of all that could prevent the power of God from reaching them through us.

Repentance is first of all God's gift to us. When we come before the Lord in sincere repentance, he releases us from the burden of guilt, depression, and despair that comes from our sinfulness. In order to receive any gift, we must reach out and accept it from the giver. We cannot receive God's forgiveness if we are too proud to accept it as the free gift it really is. Nothing we can do could ever earn this forgiveness. Many of us have experienced a sense of shame after we have sinned, knowing that we have fallen and cannot get up without help. All the more reason, surely, to turn to God and accept his gift of repentance; anything that diminishes our pride and vanity is worthwhile.

Many Christians still feel burdened and bound by their sinfulness, even after sincere repentance, because they cannot easily accept the fact that God does not expect us to become perfect overnight. This is a powerful weapon in Satan's armory. If he can tie the army of God up in knots, preoccupied with its own shortcomings, his battle is less difficult. As intercessors, we are at the forefront of the struggle against evil and its work in the world. We cannot pray for light to penetrate the darkness in others' lives if we do not allow that light to permeate us first. If we understand that repentance is indeed a divine gift, one which will set us free from our self-imposed bonds of sin, then our ministry will flower.

Secondly, repentance is not a subjective emotional experience. It is an objective reality which is not affected by our feelings. The New Testament Greek word for repentance is *metanoia,* meaning a change of heart, a change in the direction of our lives. The action of repentance is an indication of this alteration of course: we turn away from the darkness of our sins towards the forgiving and cleansing light of Christ. We should accept this in faith, and use the Word of God and its promises of forgiveness to challenge and subdue our feelings of guilt.

Repentance, correctly understood, is at the very core of intercessory prayer. All of the world's problems can be traced back to sin in one form or another, either the actual sin of individuals or nations, or the original sin of Adam. Therefore, our intercession for others cannot simply confront the physical, mental, and spiritual problems that they face. We must also address their need to realize the nature of the sin which is the direct or indirect cause of their difficulties; and how are we to do this if we are not aware of the meaning of repentance in our own lives? How can we pray for them to be given the grace to accept the gift of repentance if we do not accept this gift ourselves?

In praying for others to be led to repentance, we have no right to sit in judgment over them or to condemn them. As St. James says:

He that . . . judges his brother, speaks evil against the law and judges the law. But if you judge the law, you are not a doer of the law but a judge. There is one lawgiver and judge, he who is able to save and to destroy. But who are you that you judge your neighbor? (Jas 4:11b-12)

Thus, our intercession should not seek to specify the sins of those for whom we pray. We should rather pray that God's mercy would show them their sin, and that he would give them grace to accept his gift of repentance.

Such intercession especially applies to those who commit sin, but refuse to acknowledge it. Christ died in order that all men might be saved and redeemed from sin; but there are many who will not admit that they do wrong, and who reject any thought of guilt or responsibility for their actions. They justify their way of life by saying that they are "looking for self-fulfillment," or "achieving personal happiness and equilibrium." Even more serious is the situation of those people who *willingly* commit sin, in order to publicly assert their "liberation" from what they scornfully describe as "old-fashioned and outdated moral codes." What is to become of such people? We cannot judge their ultimate fate before the throne of God, but we should earnestly intercede for them, that they might be given the grace to understand what they are doing to themselves and others, and to turn to God in humility and repentance.

SEVENTEEN

The Intercessor
as Missionary

H OW CAN AN INTERCESSOR, whose main activity is prayer and not evangelization, be considered a missionary? In the sense of active mission work, he is not; but intercession is the most important link between the men and women who are spreading God's word, and the body of Christ, which has sent them out as its representatives.

We've already compared the ministry of the intercessor to the job of an irrigation channel. A gardener at work on a seedbed, who has bought his seeds and planted them in the soil, must watch over them and water them, so that they may bear fruit. A missionary works in much the same way. He tends the seeds of faith that God has provided for and planted in the hearts of men, nourishes them with God's word, and looks forward to the day when his efforts will bear fruit. In all of this, the intercessor is the missionary's indispensable assistant.

Before the seed has a chance to grow, it must be planted in fertile soil. In the same way, the gift of faith cannot take root unless the hearts of men are prepared to receive it. The physical circumstances of the person should be taken into account; but Jesus, during his life on earth, did not seek to improve the conditions of life of those to whom he preached. He chose instead to touch the hearts of his audience with his divine truth, and to bring about a change of heart. The intercessor has a vital role to play in preparing the hearts of nonbelievers for this change. Constant prayer focuses the grace of God on these people, and this grace effects the transformation that is necessary if they are to respond in acceptance and faith when the Good News is brought to them.

Seed that has begun to grow must suffer no harm until it is able to stand alone. The seedbed must be weeded, watered, fertilized, protected against outside interference. So, too, the newly converted Christian needs careful guidance to achieve an adequate level of spiritual maturity. While the missionary must provide this attention, the intercessor is still necessary. Prayer support for the new Christian will strengthen his faith, help him to overcome obstacles to growth that emerge, and protect him against the attempts of the devil to lead him astray or to bring him to abandon his new found faith.

In his letters, St. Paul never fails to ask his readers to pray for him and for his ministry. The Catholic Church has also emphasized this link through its recognition of the patron saints of missionaries and missions work. One is St. Francis Xavier, a priest who did splendid work in the Far East, and was one of the most successful missionaries of all time. The other is a Carmelite nun, who never left her convent from the time she joined it until her death in her early twenties: St. Therese of Lisieux. The church acknowledges that her example of constant prayer and intercession and her simplicity of faith are indispensable to the work of the missionary.

Intercessors can act as missionaries to each other. Because all those engaged in the ministry of intercession are missionaries behind-the-scenes, intercessors should identify themselves with those awaiting evangelization, so that our prayer can be more effective. We should pray for each other, that our own hearts may be aware of man's need for God, and that we may experience the hunger and thirst of mankind for truth. In this sense, we pray that the hearts of all intercessors may be fertile soil for God's word, and that we, too, may receive the

Good News afresh every day. If every intercessor were to spend a few minutes each day praying that every other intercessor might experience the newness of life of the Holy Spirit that day, the results would be quite staggering.

In his encyclical letter, *Evangelization in the Modern World,* Pope Paul VI stressed that the whole Church was missionary in essence, and that evangelization was a fundamental duty of all God's people. Within the overall evangelistic mission of the Church, her individual members have different tasks to perform. Priests and members of religious orders have the task of building up the community of the church from within, as well as missionary activity; but the primary responsibility of the laity is to use every possibility for evangelization in their everyday lives. In this activity, intercession is an indispensable spiritual foundation and support. By our intercessory activity, we participate in the missionary essence of the Church in a way that is as important as the task of those at the forefront of missionary endeavor.

Even while missionaries seek more converts to Christianity, all those who already claim to belong to the Body of Christ need to come to a genuine personal commitment to Jesus Christ as Savior and Lord. This is an even more difficult missionary field than the preaching of the gospel to unbelievers. Many so-called Christians are really only warming the church pews on Sundays. What faith they have has virtually no impact at all on their way of life. To bring about a more genuine acceptance of a Gospel lifestyle, we need to pray for all pastors, ministers, and priests, as well as for all those lay people working with them to renew their local churches. In the present situation within the Church, evangelization should be one of these persons' highest priorities. We can also play an important part in this process of church renewal through the example of our own lives.

A problem that many active missionaries and pastors face is that their time is in great demand. These people are simply unable to set aside a couple of hours each day for personal prayer. One of the primary tasks of contemplative religious orders is to pray for those people who have insufficient time to pray for themselves. Intercessors everywhere should take to heart that our spiritual "covering" of active Christian workers can supplement their own, necessarily shorter prayers. We should also pray that they be able to find more time for prayer. The pastor and evangelist St. John Vianney once said that the greater his workload became, the more time he found necessary for personal prayer. We can pray that all Christians be able to follow his example, and that their present prayer lives might be more fruitful so that they may derive greater benefit.

All Christians are called to a missionary life and witness. I've found it helpful to remind myself daily that "I am a missionary, appointed and called by the Lord to spread his word this day through my words, work, and general example." If we live in this constant realization, our lives will soon reflect it in everything we do, as the Holy Spirit moves in us. Every intercessor should look to his own local church or diocese, and support in prayer those workers and leaders who are heavily committed in the various activities of the Body. In this way intercessors will truly be the backbone of the Body of Christ.

EIGHTEEN

Practical Hints for Productive Prayer

To close our study of the ministry of intercession, I would like to share a few practical hints for those trying to develop their own intercessory prayer technique. Each person must find the approach to intercession that best suits his or her own personality, current prayer life, and level of spiritual maturity; these hints may be of value in this process.

1. *Never neglect the praise and thanks due to God.* The authors of scripture were well aware that their prayer was only possible through divine grace, and they always gave thanks and praise to God in even the darkest moments. We are called to follow their example, and always to praise God for his presence and love. Our intercession cannot fail to benefit from this positive approach.

2. *Learn to be silent within yourself.* We are surrounded by a society that cannot abide silence. Everywhere we go, we hear the noise of traffic, conversation, music, construction work—the list is endless. Many of us are afraid of being silent, without anything to take up our attention, because at times like these we cannot avoid confronting ourselves and the Lord. We need to learn to cherish these times, and to focus on God when we have learned to detach our minds and hearts from the distractions all around us. This effort will not be accomplished

overnight, but will continue all our lives. If we persevere in our efforts, and seek God's help, we shall begin to experience this inward stillness, where all that matters is to be present to God and where he is present to us.

3. *Words aren't always necessary in prayer.* In the early stages of our prayer life, we use words freely, in our native language, in song, or in tongues. As we mature in prayer, we may come to a point where we have no words that can adequately express the need we wish to pray for, or which are able to convey the depth of our feelings. At times like these, we see how limited we are by our vocabulary. God, however, existed before a human word was spoken; and he lives now within the hearts of us all. We can turn inward, and find him there; we can look to heaven, and find him there also. We are surrounded and infused by his being. In this all-embracing presence, we need no words. Let our hearts gently become one with his, and let them speak together in the silence of total unity and peace.

4. *Don't be afraid to pray in images.* There are occasions when we are deeply moved or agitated by our feelings about what we pray for. At such times it is difficult to express our confused thoughts clearly. We should remember that the Holy Spirit will read the true intentions of our hearts and convey them to the throne of God. I have found it helpful to hold an image of the person, situation, or event before the Lord. He already knows the need better than I; all I have to do is to keep it in the light of his presence through my prayer and intercede for the image in my mind. God has given us an imagination for our own good; we need not be afraid to use it.

5. *Identify yourself with the cause for which you intercede.* We cannot pray effectively if we sit as dispassionate judges. Jesus Christ did not bring salvation to mankind by remaining aloof; he chose to come among us as one of our own human race, to share our burdens, and to offer us salvation by sharing our experience of life and death. If we are to pray for the needs of others, we should be able to feel their needs as if they were our own. This might involve us in a deliberate personal experience

of the trials of others. If I want to understand the pain of starvation that so many are experiencing throughout the world, what better way to do this than by going on a fast? This will not be as severe as starvation, but will show me something of what many of my fellow men are experiencing daily.

6. *Do not be afraid of allowing your emotions into your prayer.* God has given us the gift of emotion, and we should not neglect it during intercession. While we should not become overwrought or hysterical, our prayer will be grossly unbalanced if we have a dispassionate, totally objective approach to intercession. If my brother is in pain, I feel deep personal anguish over the suffering he is experiencing, and this anguish will influence my prayers for him. St. Paul tells us to "rejoice with those who rejoice, weep with those who weep" (Rom 12:15). We are not machines, but flesh and blood; and our God-given love for our fellow man should lead us to a natural and healthy balance between objectivity about his present circumstances, and an emotional, experiential realization of what he is experiencing in them.

7. *Have expectant faith and the boldness to approach God without fear.* Jesus promised that if we ask anything in his name with all that this implies, our prayer will be heard and answered. We need not fear that God is not interested in our prayer. No matter how great or how small the object of our intercession may be, the Lord is always ready to hear us. After all, a God who is interested enough in us to count the number of hairs on our heads (Mt 10:30) will surely be interested in even the smallest needs that we bring to him in prayer. St. Paul assures us that "we have boldness and confidence of access" to Jesus (Eph 3:11-12). In this confidence, we need not be timid or shy.

8. *There will be times when we do not know how to pray.* There are times when we are simply unable to discern God's will as to how we should pray. This can be for a number of reasons: perhaps we have not taken enough time to attune ourselves to his presence, or we're agitated because of recent events and

cannot achieve the necessary inner stillness to hear him clearly, or we may be in a time of spiritual dryness. If we obtain no discernment, we should simply hold the object of our prayers before the Lord, and trust him to do what is necessary. Some like to pray in tongues; others to be silent in prayer; still others prefer to hold an image in their minds. Whatever we do, we can be sure that our very action of coming before the Lord in intercessory prayer—even if we can find no inspiration—will bear fruit. God honors our faithfulness, and is not bothered by our negative feelings.

9. *Use scripture as a source of prayer.* There are many prayers to be found in the Bible which can be applied to our own situation. Paul offers many prayers for those to whom he writes. I have found it of great help to use these prayers, putting the name of the person for whom I am praying in place of those that Paul uses, and offering these prayers to God. This technique of prayer is particularly useful in long-term intercession for someone. Our own spontaneity can dry up, and we may find that we have run out of ideas for expressing ourselves in daily prayer. These biblical examples provide a refreshing alternative.

10. *Set God free.* Our prayer should not seek to explicitly direct God as to what action to take. He is the Lord, and we his servants. Our prayer should be made after careful discernment of, and in accordance with, his will; but even then it should not seek to pin down every last detail. For example, to pray for a forthcoming missionary outreach one could use terms like these: "May this outreach be blessed by you, Lord, and may your kingdom prosper through it. May it touch the hearts of all those present with your truth and light." This is better than to pray, "Lord, it is your will that six hundred and fifty-three people shall join our church afterwards." In these examples, who is *asking* for God's grace, and who is *telling* God what to do?

11. *Be ready to offer practical assistance to meet the needs for which you intercede.* Intercession is by no means a ministry of

prayer alone. If we have not sufficiently identified ourselves with the needs for which we pray, we can be blind to our own ability to help. However, God is not blind, and he may well say to us, "Go and use the resources that I have already given you to help in this situation! Why should I divert other members of my body to perform a task that's well within your capabilities?" Intercession is not an easy ministry, and anyone wanting a quiet, undisturbed life should not embark upon it.

12. *Take time to be alone with God for longer periods.* It is a good idea to take at least a day occasionally to spend alone with the Lord. This is not easy at the first attempt; one seems to be surrounded by distractions and temptations. Whenever the great figures of the Bible or the saints of the church really needed to hear God clearly, they went aside from their followers and their work, and sought him in solitude. We need these "desert times" alone, with nothing to come between ourselves and God. He will honor our desire to draw closer to him, and will make these times fruitful. Before starting to make these personal retreats, seek spiritual direction from your pastor or from a more experienced Christian in order to avoid serious difficulties.

13. *Find a prayer partner.* This can be any fellow Christian with whom you have contact. At times, I have maintained prayer fellowship with my brethren by correspondence when I was separated by physical distance. The advantage of such a spiritual partner is that each person can support the other in prayer and fellowship, with correction or encouragement when necessary. God did not create his church to be a gathering of individualists, but intends it to be a place where Christians can strengthen and assist one another. This is particularly important in intercession.

14. *Pray for all other intercessors.* If all those engaged in the ministry of intercession are praying for one another, then the community of intercessors within the wider Body of Christ will be constantly renewing itself under the guidance of the Holy Spirit. One is thus constantly reminded that one does not

pray in isolation, but as a member of the Body of Christ. This reminder can be of great help when we encounter periods of dryness and feelings of uncertainty in our own lives.

15. *Make a habit of regular intercession.* If we approach our intercession in a haphazard way, with no set idea of when or for how long we are going to pray, we will soon run into difficulties. Set aside a certain time each day for intercession, preferably in a place where you will be undisturbed. In this way, we get into the habit of faithful, regular prayer times. When we encounter a period of dryness in our lives, when prayer is no longer easy, the established routine will help us to remain faithful in our intercessory activity.

To conclude this study of the ministry of intercession, I pray that everything said here has been of value to readers. May the Lord move in the hearts of us all, to draw us ever closer to him and to each other; and may those whom he is calling to enter upon this ministry be given the grace to respond in faith, joy, and love.